AFTA SpringerBriefs

A publication of the American Family Therapy Academy

Founded in 1977, the **American Family Therapy Academy** is a nonprofit organization of leading family therapy teachers, clinicians, program directors, policymakers, researchers, and social scientists dedicated to advancing systemic thinking and practices for families in their social context.

Vision

AFTA envisions a just world by transforming social contexts that promote the health, safety, and well-being of all families and communities.

Mission

AFTA's mission is developing, researching, teaching, and disseminating progressive and just family therapy and family-centered practices and policies.

More information about this series at http://www.springer.com/series/11846

Teresa McDowell

Applying Critical Social Theories to Family Therapy Practice

Teresa McDowell
Graduate School of Education
& Counseling, Department
of Counseling Psychology
Lewis & Clark College
Portland, OR
USA

ISSN 2196-5528   ISSN 2196-5536 (electronic)
AFTA SpringerBriefs in Family Therapy
ISBN 978-3-319-15632-3   ISBN 978-3-319-15633-0 (eBook)
DOI 10.1007/978-3-319-15633-0

Library of Congress Control Number: 2015934601

Springer Cham Heidelberg New York Dordrecht London

Springer International Publishing AG Switzerland is part of Springer Science+Business Media
(www.springer.com)

Foreword

The AFTA Springer Briefs in Family Therapy is an official publication of the American Family Therapy Academy. Each volume focuses on the practice and policy implications of innovative systemic research and theory in family therapy and allied fields. Our goal is to make information about families and systemic practices in societal contexts widely accessible in a reader-friendly, conversational, and practical style. We have asked the authors to make their personal context, location, and experience visible in their writing. AFTA's core commitment to equality, social responsibility, and justice are represented in each volume.

Over the years, I have come to realize that though many people within family therapy give voice to the need to address larger context issues and social justice, we seldom have the theoretical background that enables us to do this work. Individual and family theories alone cannot conceptualize social concerns. This is why *The Application of Critical Social Theories to Family Therapy* is such an important contribution. Dr. McDowell introduces new and seasoned family therapists alike to theories and concepts that help practitioners recognize and address the impact of societal processes in our everyday lives and in those of our clients'. She makes ideas that often seem obfuscating and dense, clear and applicable.

I am especially grateful for the generosity with which Dr. McDowell makes visible her own socially-embedded experience. In each chapter she brings theory alive through her own life story, as well as through rich descriptions of clinical practice. Readers come to see how social location frames what is more commonly thought of as individual challenges or strengths. She suggests useful clinical guidelines and tools that make it possible for clinicians to lift the veil and identify societal structures that, though they create social disparities and have profound implications for personal and relational life, typically remain invisible and unchallenged.

This highly readable volume is just what family therapists need to help widen the lens and bring larger systems into focus. The critical social theories described in this volume provide a foundation for the progressive and just family therapy and family-centered practices and policies central to AFTA's mission. Enjoy!

Carmen Knudson-Martin, Series Editor
AFTA Springer Briefs in Family Therapy
Lewis & Clark College
Portland, Oregon

Acknowledgments

I would like to thank my amazing colleagues with whom I have previously published many topics similar to those in this text. The ideas I most value have emerged from countless hours of lively discussion. My work has benefitted greatly from Flynn's insights on patriarchy and his limitless intellectual enthusiasm. I am grateful to the editor and reviewer of this series for their thoughtful guidance. Finally, I am grateful to my children and grandchildren who ensure my life is light and playful; for whom this work seems important; and who keep me filled with hope for a better tomorrow.

Contents

About the Author

Teresa McDowell Ed.D. is a professor and chair of the department of counseling psychology in the Lewis & Clark Graduate School of Education and Counseling. Teresa's scholarship centers the integration of critical social theory in the practice of family therapy. She has written about race, social class, gender, sexual orientation, and national identity using critical race, neo-Marxist, feminist, queer and decolonizing frameworks. Much of her work focuses on international family therapy in our contemporary world where economic, political, and social systems routinely contribute to increasing global inequity. As an educator and clinical supervisor, Teresa encourages recognizing and challenging power inequities that are foundational to mental health and relational problems.

List of Figures

List of Tables

Chapter 1
Critical Decolonizing Theories in Family Therapy

It has taken time to get to the ideas presented in this volume and to be able to articulate them. Like most family therapists, I started out with a deep commitment to diversity but no systematic framework for understanding the relationship between difference and power or how social systems really impact our lives. I was more aware of diversity when it was visible in the therapy room, embodied or expressed by clients (e.g., race, nation of origin, religion). I under attended the ways in which all of our daily lives are shaped by social, economic, historical, and political contexts. For example, while practicing in a wealthy suburb of a large city I saw a European American, heterosexual couple that constantly fought over money. They had a beautiful new home that needed landscaping and furnishings. The husband traveled an hour each way into the city for work and the wife stayed home with their two young children. She needed to have the home and grounds completed to begin to feel as if she fits into the planned community in which she spent the majority of her time. He felt pressured having already overstretched their budget to buy the home. He also felt trapped in a high-stress job and long commute, all without being able to satisfy his wife's expectations. I helped the couple communicate, share emotions, talk about gender roles and power differentials, negotiate money, and needs—all the typical things we do as couple's therapists. But what more could I have done?

Eventually, I found myself looking outside the field for answers to growing questions about the impact of social context on families. I gravitated to and eventually embraced the critical social theories. After years of considering how to apply these ideas to family work, I have come to believe that critical and decolonizing theories can provide family therapists with a set of lenses with which to better understand and help families navigate the social, economic, cultural, and relational realities of their lives. I share critical reflections of my own life and family therapy practice throughout this volume to demonstrate points and to link self of the therapist social awareness with the practice of critical decolonizing family therapy. I use the phrase critical decolonizing to reference recognizing and challenging processes of systematically privileging cultural, social, and economic well-being of some groups at the expense of others.

© American Family Therapy Academy 2015
T. McDowell, *Applying Critical Social Theories to Family Therapy Practice*,
AFTA SpringerBriefs in Family Therapy, DOI 10.1007/978-3-319-15633-0_1

In this volume I consolidate many of the ideas my colleagues and I have proposed elsewhere and introduce a number of critical perspectives not previously entertained. I want to acknowledge here from the start that Western thought heavily influences critical social theory. There are many other ways of knowing the world that are admittedly not considered beyond being inferred by the use of decolonizing theories. In this chapter I lay some of the groundwork for critical decolonizing approaches to family therapy. I consider how therapy can be both liberatory and oppressive; explore the basics of critical social and decolonizing theory; and integrate critical and postmodern perspectives of power. I include human rights as a special topic to challenge reliance on relativism when faced with inequity in the practice of family therapy.

Critical Social Theory

According to liberation psychologist, Martin-Baro (1994, p. 19) "…the concern of the social scientist should not be so much to explain the world as to transform it." Social theorists in general seek to understand social phenomena. Critical social theorists share this focus, but many of them also imagine what should be. For example, Marx not only focused on the inherent contradictions of capitalism, but suggested socialism as a preferred alternative. Watts et al. (2003) argued that liberation "requires vision—a transition from critique to creativity… [and]… involves challenging gross social inequities between social groups and creating new relationships that dispel oppressive social myths, values, and practices" (p. 187).

The aim of critical social theorists is to critique and influence the direction of modernity, i.e., systematic attempts to discover universal truths through scientific methods and Western oriented logic. While postmodernists question modernity itself, critical theorists question the failings of modernity to create a just society. Critical theorists acknowledge the material consequences of social constructions. For example, critical race theorists readily acknowledge that race is socially constructed. In the USA, this social construction serves to promote the economic and social power of whites. Critical theorists accept that a physical reality exists and share a value stance of supporting social and material equity. To assume otherwise would be to turn a blind eye to the very real consequences of unequal distribution of wealth and power; e.g., health disparities, global patterns of poverty. Critical theorists also consider how our social position influences our views of reality and our access to resources. For example, a white, US born, heterosexual male is likely not only to experience and describe the world very differently from a female bisexual immigrant of color, but to also have greater opportunities for securing influence and material resources.

Decolonizing theory also critiques the modern project viewing it as supporting colonial initiatives. Colonizing processes privilege the social, cultural, and symbolic capital of colonizers over the colonized leading to marginalizing and devaluing indigenous life ways (McDowell and Hernandez 2010). Economic capital and technology are often used as proof of superiority; to demonstrate greater "development" of one culture over another. Knowledge is only legitimated when produced by colonizers and is constructed in ways that "prove" superiority of those in power. For example, herbal medicines have been used for thousands of years throughout Asia yet in the Western world they are not considered legitimate treatments until/unless there have been (Western) scientific studies of their effectiveness. These studies typically take indigenous practices and healing methods out of context for examination.

Colonizing is sometimes exemplified in the practice of family therapy via the privileging of evidence-based manualized models for broad cross-cultural application, the transplantation of Western family therapy concepts and techniques to non-Western countries, and the norming of family functioning using Western ideals. Colonizing reaches far beyond one country or people dominating over another. Colonizing processes occur within cultures when those who are most powerful and dominate impose beliefs, ideologies, and expectations onto others to maintain power and privilege. For example, capitalist companies market products across groups within and among nations manipulating and exploiting the values and desires of those they hope to influence. Think of commercials that equate an automobile with sex, a laundry detergent with effective mothering, or beer with friendship. Consider what is and is not taught in history classes in primary schools and who controls this curriculum. Think about what is expected during a job interview in relationship to white middle class ways of being and relating. Last, but not least, consider how dominant, middle, and upper class, US ideals shape the everyday practice of family therapy.

Modernity, Postmodernity, and Family Therapy

Modern structural functional, critical social, and postmodern theories historically contributed to, and continue to influence the practice of family therapy. Systems theory was born out of the modern era, being applied by Bertalanffy to open systems in biology and cybernetics. Many family therapy models emerged from modern functional thought including Bowen's systems theory, psychodynamic family therapy, structural family therapy, strategic family therapy, cognitive behavioral family therapy, and emotionally focused therapy. Feminist (critical) theorists challenged the modern neutrality claims of systems theory significantly shifting the way we think about power and therapeutic systems. A number of models followed this critical movement including feminist family therapy and the cultural context model. More recently, postmodernists have suggested discarding modern-based systems altogether in favor of social constructionism (e.g., Narrative family therapy, collaborative family therapy, solution focused therapy). These major paradigm shifts build on and attempt to correct rather than simply replacing what existed before. In practice, systems theory now lives alongside postmodern, social constructionist, and critical approaches to family therapy.

Michel Foucault (1972) challenged metanarratives that make truth claims based on universal underlying structures. From a postmodern view, systems theory and critical social theories are among these metanarratives. Postmodern critiques evolved from existential traditions and have had a tremendous positive impact on the practice of family therapy. While Foucault rejected being labeled, the family therapy models we often refer to as postmodern rely heavily on his work (e.g., White and Epstein 1990). Reliance on relativism at the expense of reality claims can, however, be problematic when dealing with the material realities of people's lives (Ife 1999). Postmodern critiques themselves can inadvertently become meta-narratives, particularly when used as descriptions of the nature of reality.

For me, the crux of critical family therapy is the ability to hold space for modern, critical, and postmodern perspectives that can be used to support just relationships. For instance, when working with clients battling depression I want to be able to explore modern knowledge of brain chemistry and use research that suggests things like the ideas that exercise and sleep are likely to help. I want to track patterns of interaction around the depression and include multiple family members in therapy. I also want to be able to view, the problem with a critical lens to consider relational power differentials and overpowering social systems as contributing factors. Furthermore, I want to be able to consider dominant oppressive discourses that may be fueling the depression and shaping relationships. The goal as I see it is to integrate postmodern and systemic models of family therapy with critical social theories and decolonizing practices in ways that directly address and challenge power dynamics contributing to mental health and relational problems.

Critical Theories in the Practice of Family Therapy

Placing families within large societal systems is not a new idea. Early in the development of family therapy, Auerswald (1968) suggested an ecosystemic approach that challenged the broadly held belief that individuals and families on low income are solely responsible for their problems. Structural and strategic therapies center hierarchy and power imbalances respectively as core to family problems and symptom resolution. A number of family therapy models have conceptualized symptoms within social contexts and developed strategies for intervening across multiple systems, including multisystemic therapy (Henggeler et al. 1992) and multidimensional family therapy (Liddle 2010). The cultural context model (Almeida et al. 2007), just therapy (Waldegrave and Tamasese 1994), feminist family therapy (e.g., Prouty Lyness and Lyness 2007), and socio-emotional relationship therapy (Knudson-Martin and Huenergardt 2010) are examples of models that integrate critical theory, centering the goal of relational equity as core to therapeutic success.

Critical and decolonizing theories offer ways to understand power dynamics within and across structural contexts as well as how influence and access to resources are unevenly secured, exchanged or lost (Garcia and McDowell 2010). These perspectives require a multiocular lens that allows family therapists to consider broad social, political, and historical realities while intervening in individual, family, local "here and now" context dynamics. The threads that hold the multiplicity of critical approaches together and inform the practice of family therapy considered in this work are (1) engaging in dialectics, i.e., seeking to expose truths through dialogues of difference that attempt to resolve conflict inherent in opposing ideas, (2) critiquing social arrangements to not only describe and understand mental health and relationship problems, but to create therapeutic change, and (3) holding the belief and value position that oppressive relationships harm individuals, couples, families, and communities and should be challenged in favor of equitable ones.

Power

In her recent article entitled *Why Power Matters*, Knudson-Martin (2013, p. 6) pointed out "that the ability of couples to withstand stress, respond to change, and enhance each partner's health and well-being depends on their having relatively equal power balance." She argued, "clinical change is hard to sustain unless therapists assess for and attend to the power processes underlying... relational dynamics." These observations reflect ample evidence that relationship equity is associated with mental health and relational well-being. They also disallow a stance of therapeutic neutrality, pragmatically tying therapeutic outcomes to therapists' abilities to assess and interrupt power imbalances.

Power is frequently referred to, but rarely defined in the practice of family therapy. Critical, decolonizing, and postmodern conceptualizations of power are of particular interest to this present work. These theories share a critique of the relationship between power and knowledge, including what was viewed in the modern era as natural, universal, and true. Critical social theorists make a connection between "systems of ideas and material conditions of life" (Hick et al. 2005, p. xi), drawing attention to the role of power behind the ideology of truth claims. That is, how the powerful use rhetoric to create and sustain realities that maintain the status quo of unequal distribution of power and resources.

I am reminded of a client recently released from inpatient treatment for drug addiction. He was returning to an abusive male partner who did not support his recovery and refused to come to therapy. He frequently referenced his partner having money, a nice place to live, and standing in the community. He did so from a one-down position describing himself as lower class. He had painful class-based memories, including being ridiculed for wearing the same clothes day after day in grade school. Helping him overcome internalized classism was vital. He became better able to understand how classism functions to legitimize inequity; the way the story that the wealthy are more worthy than the poor keeps the poor believing they are inherently "less than." We drew on a lifetime of strength and resilience to promote change and therapy was largely successful. At the end of the day, however, this client was still embedded in the very real class struggles of our society. He became better prepared to navigate the class system and effectively resisted internalized classism, but his decision to choose recovery over his partner still left him needing to find adequate housing, work, transportation, and healthcare on minimum wage.

From a critical perspective, power tends to be described as relational, bidirectional, and dependent on available resources. Greater power makes it possible to prevail over another and impose one's will or objectives. Martin-Baro (1994, p. 63) relied on Weber's concept of power by defining power as "the disparity of resources that occurs in human relationships and that allows one of the actors to make his or her objectives and social interests prevail over those of others." Power is not held as a possession or intrinsic to an individual. It depends on, or resides in, the relationship between people fueled by the nature of the relationship and the resources each has to potentially bring to bear on the other. Likewise, decolonizing views of power challenge the effects of centering dominant colonizer's beliefs, values, and worldview as superior to the life ways of the colonized. These ideologies help maintain control-over while rules, laws, and social practices serve to materially benefit the colonizers.

Foucault (1972) is well known for his radically different view of power as multidirectional. He moved away from power being localized in specific situations between discrete actors with access to greater structural influence. He argued that power is everywhere. Rather than concentrated, power is diffuse. It is not held but enacted. Power is discursive, embedded in the creation of knowledge, and our understanding of what is true. Knowledge is power and the powerful have greater influence on what is defined as truth and reality. According to Foucault, power is not simply a coercive negative force, but a positive force in producing and organizing societies. Power is realized through what we believe to be real, true, and right leading us to police ourselves and each other to ensure conformity to what are often invisible social norms. For example, teenage boys are often expected by peers and older males to be interested in and willing to talk about females as objects of sexual desire. Not doing so meets with homophobic remarks and threatens male privilege. Additional examples abound. In a dominant US culture this might include the way we stand in line and disparage those who cut in front at the grocery store; the difference we might show someone who is wealthy versus not noticing someone who is poor; diets, we go on to force ourselves to become a socially prescribed size; and how we gently or not so gently discourage young girls from taking off their tops in hot weather long before they develop breasts.

Critical, decolonizing, and postmodern power analyses can be difficult to reconcile. Failing to do so, however, threatens to dismiss either the pervasiveness of dominant discourses and multidirectional power in shaping our everyday lives or underestimating the real material consequences of disparate resources that contribute to and are produced by colonization and structural oppression. I suggest that power is pervasive and unevenly distributed; systematic and idiosyncratic. Imagine power as everywhere shaping our collective and individual decisions about how to interact with each other across diverse contexts. We basically know what to expect within our cultural groups and familiar settings. We maintain social practices by policing each other and ourselves. Now imagine that power also pools up or thickens in some places; that some of us have more resources and greater influence to bring to bear in shaping singular and collective interactions. Collectively, those with greater resources and influence, shape cultural practices and ideologies in ways that benefit their own group and maintain greater access to resources. Now imagine all of this in motion with those being threatened reacting to potential and actualized power by yielding, withdrawing, navigating, and/or pushing back.

It can be helpful to consider power dynamics as both "macro" relative to broad, sweeping societal systems and "micro" relative to unique relational systems. While deeply influenced by macro embedded power dynamics, individuals within relationships still have choices and consider immediate local consequences of these choices. In fact power is often highly nuanced in intimate relationships (Knudson-Martin 2013). Those with potential power consciously or unconsciously decide whether or not to assert influence, how much, and what type of resources to use. At the local relationship level they consider the costs to the relationship, their values, how others will view them. For example, parents have a tremendous amount of power over children. Taken to the extreme they can withhold basic needs and cause severe physical harm. Parents restrain themselves from these ultimate acts of power for reasons far beyond legal consequences or the potential for children to be removed from the home. Each act of dominance over a child—of discipline—includes consideration of family values, agreements with co-parents (if applicable), impact on the child's mental and physical health, impact on a child's future behavior, and the consequences of the discipline on the relationship between parent and child.

Those with fewer resources may be trying to reduce the influence of those who have the potential to overpower. For example, discrediting one's immediate supervisor is one way to decrease the impact of her negative evaluation of your work. Others may be accommodating the powerful to avoid harm or gain power by proxy. For instance a wife may do everything in her power to please an abusive husband to avoid physical harm and family disruption. A young woman with limited resources may marry an older financially and socially successful man thereby increasing her class based influence. In other words, imagine a complex web of influence that is systematically designed to maintain power and access to resources of some over others, but is also filled with idiosyncratic, highly nuanced power dynamics in local specific contexts. It is this type of complexity we deal with daily in the practice of family therapy.

Hegemony and Professional Practice

According to Martin-Baro (1994, p. 19) "… psychologizing has served, directly or indirectly, to strengthen the oppressive structures, by drawing attention away from them and toward individual and subjective factors." This perspective can easily be extended to family therapy. While family therapy is far more contextual and pays greater attention to macro-systems than many other mental health disciplines, we have repeatedly fallen into a focus on the interior of the family as the source of pathology and/or the source of the solution.

Therapists are often placed in a position of enacting social control when clients are referred from the courts, child protection agencies, schools, and workplaces. This might include helping employees stop drinking on the job and getting kids to do their homework. Clients are sometimes seeking change to accommodate social expectations, which may in fact be for the greater good (e.g., confronting an addiction to regain custody of a child, controlling anger outbursts that harm others). Dilemmas inherent in these situations are relatively easy to see and can often be negotiated with clients and the systems in which they are involved. For example, the courts are highly influenced by recommendations of state child protection service workers. When children are removed from the home, parents are often mandated to therapy and expected to take parenting classes. When parents enter therapy, they often view the therapist as an extension of the legal and state systems that removed their children. Likewise, child protection service workers often specify goals they expect therapists to accomplish with a family and expect them to report on progress. This puts families in a bind. If they share openly with the therapist, they are potentially contributing to information that can be used against them by the state. If they do not share openly, they are considered "resistant" which can be used against them by the state.

When faced with this dilemma, I let families know that it is they who have hired me, whether paying for the sessions or not. I will communicate with state agencies and send a letter to the court only if they ask me to do so and sign a release. When I do so I will be honest and will also let them read the letter before it is sent. I warn them that I must respond to subpoenas and report when I suspect children, elders or vulnerable adults might be being harmed or if they are planning on harming themselves or others. Beyond that, my responsibility is to the family. It is up to them to decide whether or not to work on the changes they are being required to make. I coach them on how to talk to their caseworker to be certain goals are clear and achievable and/or invite the caseworker in for this conversation. I advocate and intercede in this process when the family needs and asks me to do so. Once the family makes decisions about how they want to handle the limited choices they have, we move forward in the direction they have determined and at the pace they prefer.

What is more difficult to discern is the role family therapy plays in what Antonio Gramsci called cultural hegemony; that is systems of thought and cultural practices that center and norm those most dominant in society (Jones 2006). Cultural hegemony refers to dynamics within societies where social norms and structures exert and maintain cultural dominance of the most powerful, imposing their worldviews and socio-cultural practices on the less powerful. This is part of the colonization process, which establishes and maintains the advantage of the most powerful over all others and often goes relatively unquestioned. For example, therapists may be concerned when parents report that an 8-year-old still sleeps in their bed. In the USA, children are typically expected to sleep alone from a fairly young age—sometimes from birth. I am not suggesting there is something inherently wrong with this, but that we understand this practice within a dominant culture of independence and individualism. Euro-centered mannerisms, speech patterns and writing styles, values, norms, and beliefs are often privileged in job interviews, university applications, and yes, the practice of family therapy.

There are also boundaries around knowledge such as those around professions. Professional knowledge can unwittingly be used to maintain dominant group values and privilege, serving as a colonizing force (McDowell and Hernandez 2010). For example, Schnark's argument that the pinnacle of intimacy is reached through eyes-open sex sets a sort of standard about what healthy mature adults should be able to do—look into each other's eyes while being sexually intimate or better yet while having an orgasm (Kleinplatz 2012). There is little consideration of how experts use the power of a professional position to create in this case what appears to be a heteronormed, androcentric, Eurocentric, theory-bound ideal. Very few couples actually have sex with their eyes open and fewer still look into each other's eyes while having an orgasm. As a result, you can easily find Internet blogs by those struggling with not wanting to practice eyes-open sex feeling disturbed about their newly discovered inadequacies. Likewise, therapists in the USA often place great value and belief in the self. This includes viewing the self as a reality, advising clients to take care of the self, working on raising self-esteem, and setting personal boundaries around the self. There is little consideration of self as a social construction or of who benefits from the predominant view of self. The question that goes unasked is "Who might the concept of self best serve in a late capitalist society and why do therapists find themselves accepting and promoting self as an unexamined truth claim?"

Special Topic: Critical Family Therapy and Human Rights

Modern and postmodern frameworks differ from critical social frameworks in the role of the therapist relative to social justice; neutrality being paramount in modern approaches to therapy and relativism being central to postmodern approaches. Human rights frameworks reflect what we often try to do in critical family therapy; that is supported just relationships and practices that promote mental and relational health.

Human rights are based on the concept of common humanity and principles of universality as expressed in local cultural contexts. While universal human rights have been critiqued as dominated by Western neoliberalism, they are nonetheless widely accepted and agreed upon across diverse cultural contexts. From a postmodern view, human rights might be seen as anything but universal, being socially constructed by the more powerful global forces in a particular time and place. From this perspective, can a family therapist ever declare something is wrong: that there are more or less fair and just practices within families, communities, and societies?

I argue that basic consensus on human rights is reached through what Jurgen Habermas (1985) described as communicative rationality that leads to mutual understanding. Habermas argued that through the process of communicative action, consensus can be reached that addresses what is right without requiring either absolute truth or complete subjectivity. It can be important for therapists to acknowledge at some level there may not be an absolute truth or the finite definition of what is right or wrong. Taking a relativist stance, however, leads to a false sense of neutrality. What Habermas offered is a way to think about collective wisdom and decision making. The idea being that when reasonable people come together and discuss issues such as domestic violence, child abuse, race, gender, and sexual orientation-based oppression, consensus can be reached about what should or should not be allowed across societies and cultural groups.

The postmodern era ushered in deeper respect for diversity and socially constructed cultural practices. While we have benefited greatly from these perspectives, they have also led us at times to take a "hands off" approach to widespread wrongs that are described as cultural norms. There is a tendency in helping fields to view at least some power dynamics as culturally relative (e.g., patriarchy within cultural or religious subgroups) and thereby "untouchable". When we witness genocide, systematic abduction of children, torturing of prisoners, or sex trafficking, the vast majority of us is appalled. Misuse of power is commonly understood to be problematic when it results in these widespread violations of human rights. Postmodern relativism and ontological questions of reality seem to fly out the window in the face of what resonates as simply wrong.

When family therapists work with victims of atrocity we are keenly aware that our clients have been harmed. When we witness intimate, local violations of human rights (e.g., domestic violence, sexual abuse) our ethical principles provide guidance in knowing where to stand (McDowell et al. 2012). Recognizing the terror and torture that occurs within families and communities as violations of basic human rights provides a template for discerning what is unjust regardless of culturally framed explanations. For example, male dominance and submission of women is commonplace across most of the world's cultures, often supported by religious interpretations, social systems, traditions, rituals, and cultural ideology. Violence against women, however, is a violation of basic human rights and even the most relativist of us would be hard pressed to view it as just. Looking closely at additional forms of coercive control exposes additional human rights violations such as restricting another's movements, emotional abuse, sexual force, and economic abuse (see McDowell et al. 2012 for list of specific human rights violations associated with domestic violence).

Family therapists witness daily the violations of human rights. Examples of violations that routinely occur in many countries include: poverty (i.e., basic needs and rights to safety not met); unequal educational opportunities; maltreatment of undocumented immigrants; misuse of power by social agencies and legal systems; human trafficking; legal/social disenfranchising of same sex couples; systemic racism and sexism; unlawful detainment; and sexual assault and abuse. We see these examples in family therapy along with many more subtle abuses of human rights, e.g., one partner restricting the physical movements of another, withholding basic needs from elders, pressuring partners to have sex against their will. Family therapy has traditionally considered maltreatment of family members as a matter of family dynamics and/or individual pathology rather than a more public matter of the state not upholding its responsibility to protect all citizens. This perspective supports viewing the family as private; responsible for solving problems within its interior.

Human rights discourse places responsibility for solving these issues on the state as public issues linked to structural inequalities.

A good example is the state's responsibility to intervene in domestic violence. As therapists, we are not seen as part of the state and are not held responsible for human rights conventions the state has ratified. Family therapists can, however, use a collective human rights framework to (1) guide ethical decision-making about what is right or wrong based on what most of the world agrees are basic human rights, (2) understand the social structures and cultural contexts that support denial of human rights, and (3) recognize the responsibility of, and encourage the state to intervene through laws, public policy, and funding to ensure the human rights of all citizens.

What Is Ahead?

Each of the following chapters is intended to stand alone, however, they are woven together in reference to critical social theories and reliance on interdisciplinary thought. This first chapter offered the theoretical foundation for critical family therapy. The second chapter centers on social class from neo-Marxist perspectives. Social class is addressed early in the volume, as I believe it is central to explaining all other expressions of inequity. The third chapter focuses on patriarchy. Patriarchy and capitalism are major interrelated social forces in much of the world and are referred to as such throughout the volume. In chapter four I use critical race and postcolonial theories to analyze the social construction of race, including the relationship between race and social class. Chapter five outlines structural and post-structural thought, placing family therapy models within these broad frameworks and suggesting queer theory as liberating in the practice of family therapy. Chapter six explores new ideas about applying critical geography to family therapy and offers family topography as a means of capturing power and social dynamics within the space. The final chapter is an initial attempt to articulate how critical social theory might be integrated into family therapy theory and practice.

I started this chapter with a case example: the couple arguing over money for furnishings and landscaping for their beautiful new suburban home. I have returned to that example many times in my own mind. I knew at the time that I struggled with my own biases about money and social class. But it was more than a self-of-the-therapist issue. I have been left with nagging questions that I hope to address in this volume. How did this family get into a position like this? What toll did it take on this family to work and try to live well in our economic system? How much was about living options in modern industrial cities, engaging in aggressive corporate culture, and the need to compete for intergenerational wealth? What role might I have had in helping them become critically aware of these dynamics to be better able to navigate the social systems in which they were caught?

References

Almeida, R., Dolan-Del Vecchio, K., & Parker, L. (2007). *Transformative family therapy: Just families in a just society*. Boston: Allyn & Bacon.

Auerswald, E. H. (1968). Interdisciplinary versus ecological approach. *Family Process, 7*(2), 299–303.

Foucault, M. (1972). *The archeology of knowledge*. London: Routledge.

Garcia, M. & McDowell, T. (2010). Mapping social capital: A critical contextual approach for working with low-status families. *Journal of Marital and Family Therapy, 36*(1), 96–107.

Habermas, J. (1985). *Theory of communicative action, vol 2: Lifeworld and system: A critique of functional reason*. Boston: Beacon Press.

Henggeler, S., Melton, G., & Smith, L. (1992). Family preservation using multisystem therapy: An effective alternative to incarcerating serious juvenile offenders. *Journal of Consulting & Clinical Psychology, 60*, 953–961.

Hick, S., Fook, J., & Pozzuto, R. (2005). *Social work: A critical turn*. Toronto: Thompson Educational Publishing.

Ife, J. (1999). Transforming Social Work Practice. In J. Fook & B. Pease (Eds), *Postmodernism, critical theory and social work* (pp. 211–223). London: Routledge.

Jones, S. (2006). *Antonio Gramsci*. New York: Routledge.

Kleinplatz, P. (2012). *New directions in sex therapy: Innovations and alternatives*. New York: Taylor & Francis.

Knudson-Martin, C. (2013). Why power matters: Creating a foundation of mutual support in couple relationships. *Family Process, 52*(1), 5–18. doi:10.1111/famp.12011

Knudson-Martin, C., & Huenergardt, D. (2010). A socio-emotional approach to couple therapy: Linking social context and couple interaction. *Family Process, 49*(3), 369–384. doi:10.1111/j.1545-5300.2010.01328.x

Liddle, H. (2010). Multidimensional family therapy: A Science based treatment system. *Australian & New Zealand Journal of Family Therapy, 31*(2), 133–148.

Martin-Baro, I. (1994). *Writings for a liberation psychology*. Cambridge: Harvard University Press.

McDowell, T., & Hernandez, P. (2010). Decolonizing academia: Intersectionality, participation, and accountabililty in family therapy and counseling. *Journal of Feminist Family Therapy, 22*(2), 93–111.

McDowell, T., Libal, K., & Brown, A. (2012). Family therapy and human rights: Domestic violence as a case in point. *Journal of Feminist Family Therapy, 24*, 1–23. doi:10.1080/0895283 3.2012.629129

Prouty Lyness, A., & Lyness, K. (2007). Feminist issues in couple therapy. *Journal of Couple & Relationship Therapy, 6*(1/2), 181–195.

Waldegrave, C., & Tamasese, K. (1994). Some central ideas in the "Just Therapy" approach. *Family Journal, 2*(2), 94–103.

Watts, R., Williams, N., & Jagers, R. (2003). Sociopolitical development. *American Journal of Community Psychology, 31*(1–2), 185–194.

White, M., & Epstein, D. (1990). *Narrative means to therapeutic ends*. New York: WW Norton.

World Health Organization. (2014). http://www.who.int/en/. Accessed Sept 2014.

Chapter 2
Capitalism, Social Class, and Family Praxis

As with all critical work, our own social awareness determines the degree to which we can engage in liberation-based practices with others. Our first task is to increase our own class awareness and challenge our own classism. This has not always been easy for me. I grew up in a high-status family in Flagstaff, Arizona, in the USA. While I witnessed/suffered oppression daily inside our patriarchal family, outside in the community my father's success offered us significant privilege. My father was an inventor, entrepreneur, and a community leader. He was often in the public eye. My mother entertained and smoothed the road for our family's upward mobility. It was not until I was an adult that this changed and I began to understand social class. My parents lost everything, including their home and place in the community. For the first time, a thousand miles away I had the experience of not having enough money to live on or consistently meet my children's needs. I no longer had the safety net of my parents' income and social advantage. My status was left far behind in my childhood and hometown. Still I hung on to class privilege and classism. It was not until much later after I became financially stable that I began to truly recognize and face my classism.

While social class shapes all else, the examination, explanation, and impact of social class in families are often left unspoken. Social class influences the range and types of choices available to each of us, how we define ourselves, our values and expectations, and the way we organize our day-to-day lives. Social class influences physical health, emotional/mental wellness, and relational well-being (Dilaway and Broman 2001). In this chapter, I explore social class in capitalist society relying heavily on feminist, neo-Marxist class analysis. I consider how social class is maintained, reproduced, and diminished through dynamics of social, economic, symbolic, and cultural capital. I highlight interclass families as a special topic and offer a case example to demonstrate how the concepts in this chapter can be applied in family therapy. In this chapter, social class is assumed to include a combination of education, income/financial resources, social and occupational prestige, and sociopolitical influence.

© American Family Therapy Academy 2015
T. McDowell, *Applying Critical Social Theories to Family Therapy Practice*,
AFTA SpringerBriefs in Family Therapy, DOI 10.1007/978-3-319-15633-0_2

Social Class Rhetoric

Rhetoric surrounding economic and social inequalities maintain and reproduce social class relationships. Rhetoric refers to social discourses that maintain class relationships via what Marx coined as false consciousness. Those with greater resources and power are more influential in developing and reifying rhetoric, which in turn explains, supports, and protects their social and economic advantages (Zrenchik and McDowell 2012). The "American dream", i.e., bettering oneself through hard work, is a prime example in the USA. Class arrangements and classism are justified in a land of plenty where it is assumed that anyone can make it; children can all grow up to be who they want to be. There is an assumption that no limits exist and that one person's wealth is not related to another's poverty. This is exemplified by the question "how much money do you *make*?" rather than "how much money do you *take*?" Those living on low income are assumed to be lazy or trapped in what is explained by others as a culture of poverty. Family therapists often take a liberal stance in attempts to help those in poverty, join the middle class in ways that are informed by these classist narratives. For example, a therapist may educate parents, interrupt dysfunctional patterns, or work on raising self-esteem to help families overcome poverty. If working from a solution-focused perspective, this might include identifying and amplifying times when clients felt empowered. From a structural perspective, it might be deemed important to help parents work together. From a narrative perspective, the work might involve identifying unique outcomes when family members came together and persevered. While these approaches are all likely to be helpful, they suggest at some level that those living in poverty have problems that keep them in poverty and can overcome their plight if they change their views of themselves and/or relational dynamics.

Classism is based on beliefs that those in higher classes are more worthy than those in lower classes. This is particularly insidious, as it maintains a judgmental gaze on the poor rather than on those most benefitting from the poverty and the hard work of others. In fact, the greatest admiration and respect may be shown to those who by the very nature of capitalism have garnered their wealth directly through others' hard work, or indirectly through a system in which the majority are unable to purchase without interest producing loans, need insurance to prevent economic disaster, and borrow for education to secure future income. As long as poverty is explained as the result of individual failing and wealth as the result of individual hard work and human worth, class discrimination and internalized classism will thrive.

We witness the effects of class rhetoric and the violence inherent in our social class system on a daily basis. Partners who work harder often feel entitled to greater influence in the relationship. Parents may pressure children to be involved in multiple activities including school leadership, sports, and academic clubs to secure future class advantage. Partners with higher status jobs often see themselves as superior. Extended families indirectly communicate their disappointment over a member's choice to marry below the family's collective class status. As a case in point, I worked with a mother who belonged to a parent group that got together with their toddlers once a week. She shared with me that the group often left her feeling like a bad mother; angry and hurt rather than supported. As we talked about the dynamics of the group, it became clear that members were subtly competing through their toddler's developmental milestone and social behaviors. Not only was this mother feeling unsupported, but left the group each week with nagging doubts about the eventual success of her child. Being able to talk about the impact of social class on the group's dynamics allowed her to recognize the classism she was experiencing at the hands of group members who viewed themselves as more successful (read higher class) than her. It also helped her/us to understand the fear she carried that somehow her child would not compete well in a class-based society. This understanding in turn helped head off pressure and disappointment that could have affected her relationship with her child.

Capitalism and Social Class

In a broad sense, capitalist economic systems cannot function without surplus labor, i.e., unemployment and at least some level of poverty. This keeps the marketplace balanced in favor of those with resources who can easily select and replace their workforce. More and more families are faced with unemployment, which in turn affects couple and family relationships. I am reminded of one of many clients I have seen struggling to stay just above abject poverty. This client was only able to work part time on light duty in a physically demanding, low-paying job after being injured at work. As a result, coworkers had to do more and frequently complained, questioning the legitimacy of the injury and special treatment. The union supported the worker's right to continue to work while coworkers and supervisors wanted him out in favor of their sharing needed hours and enjoying at least a portion of available light duty. There were no alternative sources of income or jobs available. Therapy went on for months with a focus **on** dealing with resulting stress and depression, finding ways to continue to enter a hostile workplace, strategies for combating the scramble for resources among overtaxed coworkers, and seeking legal support for worker's rights. As exemplified in this situation, capitalism requires that there are fewer jobs than those seeking employment. The competition for hours was the primary source of stress. Capitalism also depends on adequate demand and ability to consume what is produced as well as potential for capital expansion and reinvestment (i.e., new products and markets). Pressure for adolescents to have expensive clothes to fit in or for families to find housing that meets their developmental needs are examples of the effects of these dynamics on the everyday lives of families we see in therapy.

It is important to get a bigger picture of economic context in which we, and our clients, live. Approximately, 15 % of people living in the USA are living under the poverty line while 20 % of the population owns nearly 90 % of the wealth (Wolff 2012). In 2010, 20 % of households in the USA averaged earnings of under $ 20,000 a year and carried a negative net worth (Wolff 2012). The economic security of the vast majority rests on the ability to work; to sell their labor week to week. Poverty is a very real threat the majority of workers face; should they not be able or willing to participate in this system? Many who are not allowed to participate in the established system work without regulation or protection, constituting an underclass. For example, I worked with a family in which the primary wage earner had been in prison. He and his partner entered treatment due to the effects of prison trauma on his psychological well-being and their relationship. His record made it difficult to secure work that paid enough to support his large family. The couple did not disclose their source of income, paid in cash, and only alluded to the many stressors that appeared to originate from his work, including the fear they shared of his going back to prison. Other examples include those cleaning homes for private pay, selling products door to door for cash, picking up odd jobs in the neighborhood, and traveling to do farm work. Slave labor—which is labor that goes virtually unpaid—exists in the USA and worldwide, benefitting corporations and all of us as we consume everyday foods and products (Bowe 2008).

Families bear the burden of preparing and maintaining a workforce that sells labor to those who turn that labor into capital. This includes investments in daily shelter, food, clothing, and health care as well as long-term education, retirement funds, and child rearing. The labor that is sold is only worth what it can produce in the moment. For example, I worked with a mother who sold her labor and expertise as a nurse. Her parents had paid for her nursing education and she supported her family through this relatively well-paid profession. As the sole provider for her children, her labor and expertise had to be delivered to the marketplace (private for profit hospital) daily. She eventually became ill and was unable to sell her labor. As a result, she and her children moved across country to live with her parents where they entered therapy to deal with intergenerational conflict. The burden of caring for this mother's (laborer's) needs ultimately rested on the family in spite of their desire to enter older age with some economic security and personal freedom.

Families living in advanced capitalism are pressured to increase both consumption and participation in the labor force. Many family relational problems occur as a result. For example, children refusing to complete homework may put the well-being of the family at stake as education is an avenue for securing a well-paid position that mediates the potential for living in or near poverty and/or spending a lifetime engaged in unrewarding activity. While this is rarely articulated, it is a common experience for families to develop power struggles and other parent–child problems surrounding children's academic, athletic, community, artistic, and other performance. Couples often argue over money when surrounded by media and peer pressure to spend more, have more, and do more. Adults may feel pressured to work overtime to provide for the family while simultaneously feeling guilty for not spending more time with children. When we treat families with these struggles we rarely help them unveil the power and resource dynamics inherent in class-based, late capitalist societies.

Democracy and capitalism have been tied together as positive forces in the push for global capitalism, yet there is inherent tension between these economic and political systems (McLaren and Farahmandpur 2001). Democracy assumes potential for equal participation and opportunity, while capitalism relies on class divisions and unequal distribution of wealth and influence. The myth of meritocracy (that the USA is the land of limitless opportunity in which anyone can make it through hard work) reconciles this dilemma by blaming those most disenfranchised for their own misfortune. In fact, according to Harvey (2001, p. 121), "capitalism has … always thrived on the production of difference." Think of single mothers on welfare. These women have often fled abusive relationships or been abandoned by the fathers of their children. They are expected to take care of their children and work—to pull themselves up—being most often blamed for their plight. I am reminded of a mother I worked with one who had liberated herself and her children from a violent male partner. She lived (hid from her ex-partner) in a small, very rural community where she rented an unheated cabin. There were no available jobs in the economically depressed area. She came to therapy in crisis suffering anxiety and depression. She was going to be evicted. Her welfare check had been cut because she cut and sold firewood to make needed income. Welfare alone was not enough to live on and working to make more threatened her welfare and food stamps. In spite of her determination to provide for her children and keep them safe, she was treated as less-than by neighbors, school officials, members of her church, and welfare workers.

Global Capitalism

It is not possible to understand capitalism and social class in a given national context without recognizing what is happening globally. In January 2014, *USA Today* reported that 1 % of the global population now owns 46 % of the global wealth. Multinational corporations are replacing nations as economic units. Nations ideally have political structures aimed at securing the well-being of their citizens as a whole. Multinational corporations serve only the well-being of company stakeholders. Capitalism depends on unpaid labor and social reproduction provided by women (e.g., mother work, relational work, and housework) and below living wages of men and women worldwide. It also relies on contemporary slave labor (e.g., human trafficking, prison labor, undocumented workers, piecework) and underclass commerce (e.g., sex work, drug sales, cash work). One of the hallmarks of capitalism is continual growth, which includes constant searching for new markets within which to reinvest and increase capital (Harvey 2001). According to Harvey (2001, p. 212), "capitalism is always about growth, no matter what the ecological, social or geopolitical consequences." The power-over position of capitalism extends to the destruction of the environment, expropriation of materials and labor, and structural violence (von Werlhof 2007). This power-over framework is mirrored in relationships between men and women, humankind and the environment/animal world, and colonizer–colonized.

Colonization is closely tied to capitalism. Colonization processes center the dominant or colonizer beliefs, cultural practices, and ideologies in order to maintain advantage relative to cultural, social, and economic capital (McDowell and

Hernandez 2010). Colonizers use coercion to access the natural resources and labor (read capital) of those being colonized. In the USA, this included systematic efforts to take over land from indigenous groups (e.g., manifest destiny, imperialism, attempted genocide/assimilation, and wars to expand borders). As mentioned above, capitalism relies on surplus labor and expanding markets, which is accomplished in part through colonization.

For the most part, workers continue to be bound by location but capital is not. This means capital from the global north (i.e., economically and technically advantaged countries) can be easily transported across national boundaries and used to leverage profit from geographically bound workers in the global south (i.e., all others). Likewise, transport of raw materials and goods for consumption has become more efficient and cost-effective as space and time become less of a barrier in our contemporary world (Harvey 2001). I saw the effects of this on families in my practice in a rural lumber town. Most families I worked with had been there for generations and over time I worked with them across generations. They had historically relied on logging, lumber mills, pulp and paper mills, shake mills, shingle mills, and exportation of lumber from the local port. Most young people could enter the workforce without higher education and make as good or better income than peers with college degrees. There was a level of community pride and plenty of work. Labor costs grew high with strong unions and little excess labor. Companies began to close lumber mills in favor of shipping raw lumber overseas to be processed. Ships with logs left and ships with plywood returned. Natural recourses dwindled and environmental legislation slowed harvesting. Shake and shingle mills began closing as alternative roofing became more cost-effective. As a result, the unemployment rates soared. Families began displaying more symptoms of domestic violence, substance abuse, depression, and conflict. Suicide rates went up. A casino was constructed on a nearby native reservation and I began treating problem gambling for the first time. Without understanding the context, I would most likely have underestimated the impact of this economic and social context and sought answers only from the interior of these families.

National borders do not mark the sole divide between the global north and the global south. The global north and global south can be found in all major cities as the economic divide between the rich and the poor continues to grow. Those in the North experience more freedom of movement, safer and cleaner environments, better food, nicer housing and neighborhood infrastructures, and greater opportunity than their counterparts in the South. The global marketplace influences all families relative to work and opportunity, migration, preparation for future jobs/ education, etc. Furthermore, with the development of global media, a consumerist cyberspace has been created that is far from the lived reality of the majority of the world (Eisenstein 1998).

I am thinking about the low-income neighborhood in which we raised our children. We didn't have much, but we had more than our neighbors. We were influenced like most others by media that promotes consumerism. It was important to my sons to have a certain pair of shoes and particular coat for school. One day the neighbor boy walked home wearing my son's new coat. We were all caught in the same web. We had the advantage of being able to buy the coat, but all of us were equally influenced by the message about having to have the item to gain status and acceptance at school. I played it off as a mistake in grabbing the wrong coat to allow the boy to save face, but did absolutely nothing to change our relationship to consumerism. My view of being unquestionably in the right was severely limited by class blinders.

Social, Economic, Cultural, and Symbolic Capital

Pierre Bourdieu (1986) used a number of concepts to explain complexities of power dynamics in society, including economic, social, cultural, and symbolic capital (Garcia and McDowell 2010). Economic capital includes not only money but also capital with which to produce money outside or beyond one's own labor (e.g., income properties). Social capital refers to the network of relationships linked to the sharing of resources (e.g., being personally referred for a job, borrowing money, letters of support for school or court). Symbolic capital includes signifiers of class and status (e.g., degree titles and occupational status, family name).

Cultural capital includes assets that can be used to gain upward class mobility within specific cultural contexts (e.g., language and style of speech, skin color, looks, intellect). Cultural capital is most closely associated with the relationship between our cultural and social identities and the cultural and social identities of the dominant group or colonizers in society. Those closest to the center, to the dominant most powerful group(s), have the greatest cultural capital and typically feel the greatest sense of belonging (M. Garcia, personal communication, August 27, 2014). In the USA, this has meant privileging cultural practices, attitudes, speech patterns, values and identities that most resemble white, middle and upper class, heterosexual, able-bodied, young, conventionally attractive and masculine, English-speaking, US born males. This secures lateral advantage for those in and closely affiliated with the dominant group as well as vertical advantage as the legacies of group members are secured. Cultural capital is intertwined with social capital as networks are built in part based on reproducing in-group advantage. For example, a company may seek diversity (read non-white hires) yet choose those who most closely reflect the language use, attitudes, dress, cultural practices, and values of the dominant group. This often results in a human landscape, speckled with **dark**ened bodies, which continues to privilege the dominant group without transforming the center in ways that truly reflect valuing diversity.

Understanding the dynamics of ascending or diminishing social class requires close examination of the interconnected systems of economic, social, symbolic, and cultural capital. For example, economic security relies in part on who one knows; one's education and title; one's race, sexual orientation, gender, and birth place; conformity to dominant culture rules, laws, and practices, and so on. These are not independent of each other. Getting into school or staying out of prison may be determined by who can write letters of support. Dominant speech patterns and grammar often reflect generations of practice and formal education (or lack thereof), which has historically been based on race, gender, and social class.

According to Bourdieu (1986), we participate in social exchanges to increase and maintain social capital. Families with more resources often have a greater opportunity to maintain class privilege or ascend in social class within their lifetimes (Bourdieu 1986). In contrast, those at the lower end of the economic hierarchy are at greater risk than their upper class counterparts of descending in social class (Stanton-Salazar 2001). All families are vulnerable to losses in social capital due to loss of job, illness, legal problems, etc. Low-status families are more likely to experience loss of social capital due to social exchanges that are unproductive or diminishing. When children fail in school, act out in the community, use drugs, or engage in illegal activity, it increases the likelihood of downward mobility, particularly among families who are perched on the edge of or living in poverty without protection of well-placed social networks, symbolic capital, or cultural capital.

Garcia and McDowell (2010) developed a tool for therapists to use with low-status clients when considering constraints and opportunities across multiple systems relative to social capital. Constraints might include limited transportation, language barriers, and lack of available social supports. Opportunities might include wealth of parents, educational degrees, and religious communities. Opportunities and constraints may coexist and be in direct conflict. For example, an adolescent may gain capital in his peer group by committing an illegal act or being the best at holding his liquor. At the same time, breaking the law and drinking may constrain capital outside of the peer group. The tool tracks multiple interconnected systems in which families are embedded to explore their choices for navigating these systems in ways that can maximize social influence and access to resources.

Special Topic: Interclass Families

Some families are formed across social classes. Once a unit, these families are often grouped by others into a single status; however, the effects of class differences can have lasting effects on couple, parent, and extended family relationships. Couples may experience differences in their ideas about money; perspectives on the balance between economic stability and job satisfaction; attitudes about work, education, and social mobility; and expectations of (and by) families of origin (McDowell et al. 2013). Tensions may arise in families when the marriage of a member results in downward or upward social mobility. For example, those who move upward are sometimes seen as betraying the family of origin, no longer sharing the family's values and worldview; forgetting where they came from; and/or perceived as thinking they are better than the rest of the family. Upwardly mobile family members are often strongly loyal to their families of origin and feel obligated to help them. Marrying outside one's family's social class may also create tension in families of origin. For example, there may be a lack of acceptance of the new partner and in-laws of adult children who marry others from social classes lower than their own. Parents who have invested significant resources in education and ensuring opportunities for their children may feel shortchanged in the marital bargain.

Case Example

Sam and Patrice had been a couple for several years when they entered therapy. They described their relationship as generally warm and supportive but when differences arose they tended to feel misunderstood. Attempts to get through to each other often escalated into yelling matches followed by long periods of silence. Sam often turned to her family at these times. They listened, empathized, and agreed with Sam's negative interpretation of Patrice's points of view. Patrice kept couple problems to herself, turning her dissatisfaction inward.

Sam's family was generally accepting, but felt Sam "could have done better" in her choice of partner. Patrice's family was unaware of her sexual orientation. Patrice and Sam both identified as white, able-bodied, women who were born and lived in a progressive city on the west coast of the USA. Sam had met her family educational and occupational expectations by becoming a practicing attorney. Patrice's family turned to her for financial advice and support, which she willingly offered now that she was a certified public accountant. Patrice felt she no longer belonged and at times envied the close relationships Sam and her family shared.

When the couple described their differences, the therapist noticed a tendency for Patrice to be safety-oriented, preferring stability and predictability. Sam described herself as spontaneous, highly valuing adventure and leisure time. Patrice believed work should be done before play. Sam believed the exact opposite. Patrice's life experience had led her to be conservative with money and prioritize earning over spending. Sam's experience led her to have a sense that there would always be an economic safety net and that it was important to enjoy life, not just survive. Patrice saw Sam as irresponsible. Sam thought Patrice was controlling. Sam was frequently angered by Patrice's fear of coming out to her family. Patrice worried that Sam would out her without permission.

Patrice's family was proud of her achievements but also consistently inferred that Patrice felt she was now better than the rest of them. Patrice defended her family and felt obliged to make sure their needs were met but also felt she was in a no-win situation. Coming out felt too risky to an already strained connection. While Sam met many of her family's expectations, Patrice and her family were not at all what they had envisioned for Sam's future. The couple's relationship to money, security, work, and play reflected their differences in social class background. Sam assumed they would always be able to recover financially if a risk did not pay off or their bank account was tapped for a vacation. Patrice struggled to spend time or money on what was not necessary and wanted to downplay their ability to do so.

Social class might be missed among the many factors contributing to this couple's struggles. Furthermore, therapeutic conversations regarding sexual orientation might have been limited to experiences of discrimination and homophobia as daily stressors. Considering the interplay of cultural, social, economic, and symbolic capital led to new understandings for the therapist and couple. Patrice and Sam had to continuously assess every context they entered to determine the potential impact of being out relative to cultural, social, symbolic, and economic capital. For example, when either of them had potential clients in their respective professional roles, they had to determine what aspects of their cultural capital could be shared. Exposing their sexual orientation with at least some of those in the dominant hetero-normed, homophobic, male-dominated center could result in diminished capital beyond what might be lost by being female. Their earned degrees and expertise could suffer dismissal in these contexts. Furthermore, their respective her-stories of coming out to family, friends, and communities are likely to have been influenced by relative risk associated with differences in social class.

Implications for Practice

Social class shapes all family and therapeutic systems. For example, a therapist working in a publically funded agency is likely to work with families of lower status than the therapist herself. These agencies may tell therapists not to dress too nicely so their clients would not feel uncomfortable and routinely set educational and self-esteem goals with clients in order to help them break the cycle of poverty. On the other end of the spectrum, private practitioners may wear upscale attire; ensure middle- and upper-class families have private waiting rooms; and offer operating hours that flexibly meet the needs of busy professionals. Awareness of the dynamics of social class allows us to take a meta view of the therapeutic system; to better engage in analysis of second-order cybernetics.

Therapists need to routinely assess dynamics of social class and talk about these dynamics with clients. Figure 2.1 includes a sampling of questions therapists might ask about social class. Social class awareness is liberatory—that is, it helps free us from rhetoric that maintains classism and internalized classism, freeing us to navigate our lives in more empowered, thoughtful ways. Helping clients analyze their own lives raises critical consciousness of the dynamics of power and social class so they are better able to take action on their own behalves (Freire 1970; Korin 1994; Martín-Baró 1994). As family members gain awareness of the impact of social class on their assumptions, values, attitudes, and relational dynamics, they are in better positions to act and make decisions together from more empowered perspectives.

1. Where and what did each of you learn about the meaning of money? Social class?

2. How has having money/not having money and/or access to employment (e.g., degrees, work experience, social status) affected your attitudes toward work? Spending? Leisure time? Social groups? Saving? Taking risks? Moving if you chose to do so?

3. What are your family legacies around social class? How did that affect your family of origin? Current family? Relationships between family members?

4. What worries or fears do you have about money? About social class? In what ways does your partner contribute to alleviating or aggravating those fears?

5. What has it been like for you to come together as a couple across the social classes in which you grew up? How do you think differences in your social class backgrounds affect things like your use of language, attitude toward certain behaviors, comfort or desire to socialize with specific groups of people, and so on?

6. What hopes do you have for your children's (if any) future financial and social success? What do you see yourself doing to secure those hopes? In what ways do you see your partner supporting or not supporting your goals for your children?

7. In what ways would you be able to rely on others/not rely on other for economic security if you were in dire need? What social influence do you and/or others have that could rely on if needed? What difference does this make to you and to your relationship?

8. How have you and members of your family who have gone before you managed hard times? What types of resilience have these times helped you develop?

9. Have you or your family moved across social classes? If so, what effect has this had in your family relationships?

Fig. 2.1 Examples of questions a therapist might ask about social class

References

Bourdieu, P. (1986). The forms of capital. In J. G. Richardson (Ed.), *Handbook of theory and research for the sociology of education* (pp. 241–258). New York: Greenwood Press.

Bowe, J. (2008). *Nobodies: Modern American slave labor and the dark side of the new global economy*. New york: Random House.

Dilaway, H., & Broman, C. (2001). Race, class and gender differences in marital satisfaction among dual-earner couples: A case for intersectional analysis. *Journal of Family Issues, 22*(3), 309–327.

Eisenstein, Z. (1998). Global obscenities: Patriarchy, capitalism, and the lure of cyber fantasy. New York: University Press.

Freire, P. (1970). *Pedagogy of the oppressed*. New York: Continuum.

Garcia, M., & McDowell, T. (2010). Mapping social capital: A critical contextual approach for working with low-status families. *Journal of Marital and Family Therapy, 36*(1), 96–107.

Harvey, D. (2001). *Spaces of capital*. New York: Routledge.

Korin, E. C. (1994). Social inequalities and therapeutic relationships: Applying Freire's ideas to clinical practice. *Journal of Feminist Family Therapy, 5*(3/4), 75–98.

Martín-Baró, I. (1994). *Writings for a liberatorion psychology*. Cambridge: Harvard University.

McDowell, T., & Hernandez, P. (2010). Decolonizing academia: Intersectionality, participation, and accountabililty in family therapy and counseling. *Journal of Feminist Family Therapy, 22*(2), 93–111.

McDowell, T., Melendez, T., Althusius, E., Hergic, S., Sleeman, G., Ton, N., & Zimpfer-Bak, A. (2013). Exploring social class: Voices of inter-class couples. *Journal of Marital and Family Therapy, 39*(1), 59–71. doi:10.1111/j.1752–0606.2011.00276.x.

McLaren, P., & Farahmandpur, R. (2001). Class, cultism and multiculturalism: A notebook on forging a revolutionary politics. *Multicultrual Education, 8*(3), 2–14.

Stanton-Salazar, R. (2001). *Manufacturing hope and despair*. New York: Teachers College Press.

von Werlhof, C. (2007). No critique of capitalism without critique of patriarchy: Why the left is no alternative. *Capitalism, Nature, Socialism, 18*(1), 13–27.

Wolff, E. (2012). *The asset price meltdown and the wealth of the middle class*. New York University. Unpublished manuscript.

Zrenchik, K., & McDowell, T. (2012). Class and classism in family therapy praxis: A feminist Neo-Marxist approach. *Journal of Feminist Family Therapies, 24*(2), 101–120.

Chapter 3
Gender and Patriarchy

As a child, I could readily see and feel the impact of male privilege and dominance. By the time I was 8 years old, I understood it to be the way things are and felt the smack of unfairness it delivers. My father loved us fiercely. He demanded compliance and used coercive means to control my mother, all of the children, our extended family, and his employees. He acted out a one-up posture with most other men in the community. In many ways he was bigger than life. My brothers were granted male privilege in the family but also suffered brutal attempts by my father to usher them into patriarchy. Having been deeply immersed in it all of my life, patriarchy has been difficult for me to really see. I have talked at length about androcentrism, male privilege, male dominance, and patriarchy. It has been only recently, however, that I have had the means, courage, and awareness to come out from behind the veil of patriarchy and realize the depth of its influence on most of our lives. This has been a gradual awakening for me at the cost of significant relationships as I have become less and less willing to participate.

In this chapter I consider the dynamics and impact of patriarchy on families. I begin with a discussion of feminism and resistance against gender oppression. I link resistance to resilience. I then explore the impact of postmodernism on feminist thought. I describe patriarchy, link gender to capitalism and social class, and explore the costs of patriarchy. I consider the impact of patriarchy on relationships between fathers and sons as a special topic followed by a case example and implications for how what is presented in this chapter can be applied in the practice of family therapy.

Feminisms

Just as resistance can consistently be found where there is oppression, male dominance and privilege have always met with resistance from women. Resistance has taken many forms across time and place. Three waves of feminism are often cit-

© American Family Therapy Academy 2015
T. McDowell, *Applying Critical Social Theories to Family Therapy Practice,*
AFTA SpringerBriefs in Family Therapy, DOI 10.1007/978-3-319-15633-0_3

ed from a contemporary Western framework. The first wave spans from the late nineteenth to early twentieth century, resulting in women's right to vote and other social and legal rights. The second wave was the Women's Rights Movement in the 1960s–1980s, resulting in women politicizing their personal lives and pressing social change toward greater equity. The third wave is from the 1990s through the present, and focuses on realizing promised change and pressing further to dismantle systems of male privilege and patriarchy. Feminism has been heavily critiqued as primarily white, heterosexual, middle and upper class women speaking for—generalizing the experiences and goals of—all women. These women and their families (including my family) are typically first to benefit from social change. For example, educated white women were first to enter better paying jobs contributing financially to white middle and upper class families. Throughout this period women of color have fought for equal rights not only with men, but with white women. Black and Chicana feminisms are examples of social movements that challenge race and social class along with gender. The conflation of race, class, and gender, as well as the privileging of white feminism was captured by hooks (2000, p. 19) who asked "[in] white supremacist, capitalist, patriarchal class structure, which men do women want to be equal to?"

While these waves have had a significant impact on women's rights over time, it is important to recognize and acknowledge the everyday, every place resistance of women to male dominance. Resistance is often written out of history in favor of portraying the oppressed as helpless and able to be completely overpowered. Resistance may only be noticed when masses rise against oppressive forces, when in fact resistance is an everyday occurrence found everywhere. Afuape (2011) argued aspects of everyday resistance include the ways people always resist oppression; the ways we all struggle with contradictory positions and ways of responding to oppression that can coexist; the back and forward movement toward liberation that is forever shifting and changing; the place of our relationships and social circumstances in supporting or constraining movements in our preferred direction; and the possibility of being both oppressor and oppressed. (p. 72)

This is important in relational therapy as resistance is often misunderstood, pathologized, or goes undetected as a source of strength. Everyday resistance is frequently overlooked which lessens the opportunity to pass strategies of resistance across generations. For example, my grandmother was forbidden by my grandfather to, among other things, speak her native language. What I noticed is that she rarely spoke at all except for her whispers of resistance to me as I got older about grandpa and her life as we sewed, cooked, and chatted together. My mother was under my father's control when he was present. When he was not she was lively, fun-loving, and relaxed. Her resistance came in many forms including her spirituality, failure (read refusal) to clean the house, and hours spent as a musician. Her resistance was also sometimes costly resulting in medical problems, emotional breakdowns, and eventual alcoholism. While times have changed, I still learned from my mother and grandmother about the power of sometimes not speaking, the importance of maintaining free space, and the cost of staying in relationships that require physical and mental sacrifice to balance power. I also learned about the depth of resilience in the human spirit as my grandmother quietly went about writing a book on local history and my mother went to college in her 50s, committed to recovery, and liberated herself and our family through divorce.

I have come to recognize that resistance is closely tied to resilience. The act of resistance itself often contributes to resilience. How we learn to resist oppression may help us bounce back after we experience life struggles and trauma. Resistance is not without cost. I am suggesting here, however, that we look for and amplify the resilience that resistance often promotes alongside or beyond its emotional and relational costs. For example, I have worked with many women and children who learned to accommodate a powerful patriarch—to attend to his body language, mood, and needs; to hold steady in the face of anger; to proactively seek safety; to care for and protect each other; to hold on to spirituality in the face of brutality. Recognizing this resilience—how they were able to endure, to overcome—and using it to move forward has been the focus of many conversations in therapy.

Feminisms and Post-Structural Thought

Debates regarding the fit between postmodern/post-structural and critical/feminist theories are not new, yet unresolved tensions remain which at times detract from our ability to integrate these frameworks in ways that benefit the goals of social equity. As noted elsewhere in this volume (see McDowell, Chap. 1), modern approaches to change focus on reforming social structures, working toward developing more equitable social arrangements. In the case of feminist/womanist social movements, shared (albeit diverse) female identity provided a basis for solidarity necessary for group action. According to Morely and MacFarlane (2012):

> Feminism is a modernist emancipatory project, predicated on the construction of a particular political agenda pertaining to a grounded subject or particular identity (i.e. woman) and a grand narrative espousing a 'truth' about how patriarchy oppresses women. Because, from a feminist perspective, the gendered oppression and exploitation of women are morally wrong, changes must occur in order to end such oppression. (p. 72)

Post-structural frameworks reject universal, categorical identities. This dispels generalizations about a universal nature of sex and gender. The popular book *Men Are from Mars and Women Are from Venus* is a prime example of assuming there are two discrete sex categories complete with gender-linked attitudes and behaviors. Many of those with whom we work have compared themselves and others to these types of essential, categorical differences between males and females. I am thinking of a girl I worked with some time ago before being introduced to post-structural thought. Among other gender variant behavior, she wore male identified clothing and got into fistfights at school. I remember struggling to categorize her in my own mind: Was she a tomboy? Was she transgender? What I was unable to do is help her and her family dismantle these categories in favor of supporting this young person in developing and expressing who she wanted to be. At the same time, as an identified biological female, she had the right under Title IX to be treated fairly without gender discrimination and with equal access to sports, etc. at her local rural school.

What I am arguing for here is the need for family therapists to hold tensions between feminist frameworks that insist on category-based social change in family life (e.g., men participating more in family life, sharing of household chores, equal decision making influence in couples) and post-structural frameworks that question the very categories upon which gender inequity is based (see McDowell, Chap. 5, this Volume). Both are liberatory. For me, these ideas have gone hand-in-hand as I have analyzed and increasingly rejected gender-based oppression and categorical gender identity.

Describing Patriarchy

Gender inequity is widespread as patriarchy is the most common principle of social organization across nations, social classes, ethnicities, and religious groups. According to the World Health Organization (2014):

> Gender determines the differential power and control men and women have over the socio-economic determinants of their mental health and lives, their social position, status and treatment in society and their susceptibility and exposure to specific mental health risks.

Differences in privilege within families create problematic power relations and lack of material necessities creates stress on all family relationships.

Patriarchy is a form of social organization in which men are centered, dominant, leading figures in social life as well as primary authorities within the family. To use Walby's (1990) words, patriarchy is "a system of social structures and practices in which men dominate, oppress and exploit women" (p. 20). This definition highlights social structures as the problem rather than individuals. Walby outlines four feminist frameworks that have grappled with understanding patriarchy. Liberal feminism focuses on rights and fairness within existing structures. This includes equal pay and employment, sexism, gender discrimination, violence against women, and related social problems, but not critiquing or attempting to dismantle overarching social structures such as capitalism. Radical feminism "is distinguished by its analysis of gender inequality in which men as a group dominate women as a group and are the main beneficiaries of the subordination of women" (p. 3). Radical feminists view male dominance as independent of capitalism. Marxist feminism does just the opposite, viewing male dominance as intertwined with and a by-product of capitalism. Male dominance replicates power over capitalist structures. Dual-systems feminists argue that capitalism and patriarchy are separate yet interconnected systems. Both are required to understand and explain gender relations. I use this dual-systems framework here in defining and explaining patriarchy.

According to Dickerson (2013, p. 109) "patriarchy puts men at the center of their experience, so that what happens in their living situation is simply for them to 'enjoy,' neither to analyze nor to be accountable for." Male influence is routinely more valued than female influence and male work is assumed to be worth more. Patriarchy goes beyond male–female relationships, however, mirroring other systems of power-over, e.g., humans over nature and animals, boss over worker. The argument that male dominance is a natural outcropping of biological, emotional, psychological, and even spiritual differences (e.g., Aristotle's view of men as perfect and women as imperfect) has been effectively challenged by feminist historians who point to the advent of patriarchy as an indicator of its social rather than "natural" basis (Lerner 1986).

Patriarchy is complex and multifaceted, affecting all of us in a variety of ways and is inherently flawed as a relational social system leading to a plethora of individual and relational problems. A Marxist practice of dialectics, which sheds light on tensions and contradictions within systems such as capitalism, can illuminate some of the binds in patriarchy. For example, patriarchs are supposed to protect, provide for, and solve the problems of others. Competence in these areas is highly valued and evaluated as individual accomplishment. There is an inherent contradiction, however, as none of these expectations are singularly within an individual's control. Protecting and providing are contextually situated and depend on access to resources, degree and type of family need, political climate, and so on. Solving the problems of others is possible when asked to do so and when problems are practical like changing a tire or entertaining kids while a partner rests. This becomes much more complex when there are no ready solutions (e.g., emotional reactions to loss) or solutions require collaboration (e.g., balancing work and home life). These contradictions often lead to nonsolutions such as attempts to control and the anger that tends to follow failed attempts to control. For example, a wife may be sad and crying over the loss of her parent, turning to her husband for support. He is likely to offer advice (try to solve the problem) in ways that fit patriarchal frameworks (e.g., "don't think about it so much," "it was his/her time"), which in turn frustrate the wife's bid for nurturance. When the problem persists after attempts to solve it fail, the husband may then get frustrated with the wife and see her as a problem. This, in turn, may reinforce the wife's patriarchy-informed view of herself as weak, emotional, and dependent. While patriarchs hold a more central position, both partners suffer from this arrangement. Patriarchs are often left unable to meet social expectations—caught in perpetual struggles for control and distant from those whom they care about most deeply. Non-patriarchal adults and children may suffer loss of personal agency, experience emotional, financial and/or physical harm, and/or struggle with a variety of physical, social, or emotional problems.

Not all patriarchy is the same and patriarchy is performed differently across families and communities. Those searching for male partnership often seek masculine yet benevolent patriarchs. For example, in some religions, including groups within Christian and Islamic traditions, male leadership is ideally tethered to service to the family, care and attention to meeting the needs of others, submission to God, and engagement in fatherhood.

Gender, Capitalism, and Social Class

Women do the majority of the world's labor, produce over half of the world's food, receive approximately 10% of the world's income, comprise 70% of those in absolute poverty, and own only about 1% of the total wealth. Capitalism generates and relies on difference (Harvey 2001) and differential power. The power-over framework of capitalism is mirrored in patriarchy, which entitles men to have power over women and children. In at least some ways, male privilege cuts through diverse advantages and disadvantages that differentiate male experience. That said, there is vast difference in men's privilege based on race, class, sexual orientation, and abilities.

Masculinity and sexism are intimately tied into these social processes. Men in most societies must continually act out their manhood. According to Beneke (1997), manhood is proven by perseverance when faced with distress. Working hard through exhaustion or pain, putting fear aside, not identifying with softer feelings, swearing, dealing with what is offensive, and exerting superiority and dominance over women as not men are a few ways masculinity is performed and defended. As a case in point, I remember my brother complaining about a task to my father who replied, "If it were easy, we'd have the women do it!" This stoicism is connected to protection and production as men are preparing to face war, take on dangerous jobs, work long hours, and compete in the workplace. Women are likewise expected to suffer. Putting the needs of others first, accommodating unequal power dynamics, and enduring male dominance are but a few expectations.

Costs of Patriarchy

Patriarchy is clearly associated with women's mental and physical health, including rates of death by homicide. In a cross-cultural study of patriarchy and health, Stanistreet, Bambra, and Scott-Samuel (2005) found as expected that the cost of patriarchy was high for women, but also costly for men's health and mortality. They echoed Freire's (1970) assertion that oppression is harmful to the oppressor as well as the oppressed.

Women have long suffered the effects of male oppression too numerous to include here, but certainly include violence and sexual assault, restriction on movement, unequal ratios of work to leisure, underpay for equal work, humiliation, and degradation. Women have been silenced, their ideas undervalued, decision making undermined, and personal agency tethered to male needs. It is not uncommon for heterosexual middle-class women to make a forced-choice bargain with patriarchy. Giving up one's potential for meaningful work and following a life course which most benefits a successful male partner comes at a cost as it often requires women to tithe power in return for social and economic benefits. I am thinking about a woman I worked with who had been married to a highly successful male partner for most of her life. After meeting in college, he pursued a dynamic career and she followed him across country with each promotion. Now in her 60s she had a beautiful home and considerable influence in the community. Her husband refused to come to therapy or to consider ending an affair. She chose to remain in the relationship and to hand over part of what little power she had as a way to secure her class and community position. In this case, as is true in many, the original bargain to be a couple and put his career first was more easily broken by the husband who later pursued a different (in this case additional) relationship. Often they take their careers with them, leaving their wives compromised by a lifetime of lost opportunities and little independent security.

Men sometimes lose important relationships due to their privilege and unwitting participation in patriarchy. For example, my practice had a constant flow of men calling in crisis after their wives left them. The story was often the same. Their wives repeatedly tried to influence the relationship to create changes necessary to be able to stay before finally giving up. Now the husband was "willing to do anything" yet it was most often too late. I almost always ask: "how long has your wife been trying to get you to go to therapy?" The question has never gone unanswered. These men whose wives walked away from patriarchy are in genuine pain—their relationships destroyed by their privilege.

Patriarchy also deeply affects men's relationships with each other (F. McDowell, personal communication, July 16, 2014). According to Pleck (2014), hierarchy exists among men who rate themselves and each other according to masculine attributes. He argued that the heterosexual–homosexual dichotomy is centered in sexual politics. Behaviors that do not conform to masculine ideas (e.g., stoicism, competition) are associated with being gay. I would add to this that the male–female dichotomy and adult–child dichotomy are also at play as non-masculine behaviors are also associated with being female and/or childlike. Pleck (2014) argued that for heterosexual men, women mediate male relationships through their cooperative relationships with each other, provide a haven for retreat from male competition, provide symbolic status as part of how men evaluate each other, and serve as an underclass that protects men from being at the lowest rung of society.

Special Topic: Fathers and Sons

Early Marxists, including Weber, pointed to the ill effects of male power over younger males (Walby 1990) and male feminists have shared numerous stories of the negative emotional effects of patriarchy (Pease 2000). During the 1970s and 1980s, concern emerged over the wellbeing and development of boys who experienced the emotional or physical absence of their fathers. This dovetailed into feminist ideals of men becoming more involved in family life and being better prepared to nurture children alongside women. In a qualitative study entitled "the father-wound," Pease (2000) described pro-feminist men's memories of their fathers being unable or unwilling to help them through emotional struggles, making demands on them around work, expecting them to be tough, and other reflections of traditional masculinity. These men described understanding women's experiences of male dominance, privilege, and patriarchy as they themselves experienced these dynamics during childhood.

One way to look at the hegemony of patriarchy is that at least some older men see themselves as having control over younger men whom they usher in, or groom, as future patriarchs. Men (and sometimes women) in families, businesses, peer groups, sports events, community groups, and the media teach boys how to be patriarchs by ridiculing them if they are close to their mothers, making misogynist and sexist remarks in all male groups, showing men how to objectify women, teaching boys to suffer through emotional and physical discomfort, displaying homophobia over non-masculine behaviors, teaching competition, and demonstrating restriction of empathy for others. I was reminded of this recently in supervision when a young male client smirked at his crying mother. When he himself admitted to feeling emotional he described himself as a momma's boy. One of the supervisees in our group told his story of growing up smirking to mask forbidden feelings in order to remain male-identified among male family members and friends. It was his way to hold back tears and compassion that were incongruent with expectations of him as a future patriarch. Many women socialize girls into patriarchy as well, teaching them how to thrive in this unjust system. Girls are taught to think of others first, forgo their own needs, and accommodate males.

Young men who grow up in male dominated, male privileged families are faced with difficult decisions. They may witness and experience the emotional and physical toll of patriarchal control. Their empathy for mothers, sisters, aunts and grandmothers becomes a liability—hence the traditional expectation that boys will not be close to their mothers and other women in the family after a certain age. They learn what it means to be on the wrong end of the power equation as they are simultaneously being promised a way out by being socialized into male privilege. They may feel pressured to be as successful, hardworking, and competent as their fathers while getting the message that their fathers are still in control. This creates a double bind in which sons cannot meet the expectations of their fathers without betraying them by overthrowing their dominance and control.

Case Example

Mark, a European American man, age 32, entered treatment for problem gambling. Mark's mother attended therapy with him at first followed by his father and brother at the therapist's insistence. Mark's mother had spent her life supporting her husband (e.g., working to put him through school, managing the household so he could work long hours, socializing in the community in ways that supported his career) and raising her children. Mark's father was a successful businessman. Mark's only sibling was an older brother who worked in the family tool dye business. Mark had worked the family business until he was caught embezzling funds from the company in order to gamble. His mother was now his primary connection to the family. When Mark and his father had occasion to talk—usually when Mark needed money—his father would offer unsolicited advice about getting a job, handling money, using time effectively, and not giving in to urges to gamble. Mark's brother echoed their father urging Mark to find someone, settle down, grow up, be a man, be responsible, and not keep relying on their parents.

Mark and his brother described their experiences being ushered into patriarchy from very different lenses. Mark's brother played sports, dated extensively, went hunting with his dad, and never understood why his mother complained so much. Mark felt pushed into playing sports and disliked the pressure he felt from his father. He often took his mother's side as he witnessed his father dismissing his mother's feelings, overrunning her decisions, and being dishonest with her about many aspects of his life.

As gender roles and the meaning of money were introduced as routine inquiries relative to problem gambling, it became increasingly clear that Mark was in an impossible bind. The less Mark's father viewed him as successfully masculine, the more his father gave him advice on how to be a man. When advice was not used, Mark's father would simply increase his micromanagement of his son. Mark could not take his father's advice in how to become an assertive, masculine, patriarch without denying himself and being subservient in his willingness to do as his father said. Mark searched for ways to be successful that were out of his father's purview. While problem gambling cannot be explained away by a few relational dynamics, it was clear that part of what maintained the gambling was Mark's focus on how his life would be different if he struck it rich. The hope of making a fortune gambling allowed him to live in a fantasy where he could have freedom to be who he wanted to be and prove his manhood on his own terms.

Implications for Practice

Knudson-Martin (2013) argued that when couples present (as most do) with unequal power in the relationship it is not possible for the therapist to be neutral. Not attending to the power imbalance contributes to it; yet working toward shared power may be seen as a therapist-driven agenda. This would leave therapists forced to choose between conflicting ethical principles if it were not for the pragmatics of power imbalances creating and maintaining relational problems. Following are a few examples of how therapists can promote gender equity.

In Socio-Emotional Couples Therapy (Knudson-Martin 2013), the therapist places power dynamics at the center of analysis with the goal of relational equity being foundational to sustainable change. Interventions aim at developing shared relationship responsibility, mutual vulnerability, mutual attunement, and mutual influence. Critical conversations (see McDowell, Chap. 7, this volume) about gender are important in exposing patriarchy and may include questions such as: Where did you each learn to be male/female? How well do you fit into gender expectations?

What are the consequences of not fitting gender expectations? What do you see in the media about gender: male control over females? Who was/is in charge of the family and why? And, in your family, how did/does gender influence expression of emotion? Media and group work can be used to raise awareness and accountability. For example, the Cultural Context Model (Almeida et al. 2007) uses media clips in men's and women's groups to raise critical consciousness around gender, power, and patriarchy. Finally, I often use sculpting when working with patriarchal families. As men stand on a stool in the middle of the room, not able to see into the faces of their families, they often get in touch with how their power-over leads to deep loneliness and separation from those whom they love the most. I have many memories of prompting men to step down from the stool and asking families to demonstrate how they will come together to include men and promote safety and equity for women.

References

Afuape, T. (2011). *Power, resistance and liberation in therapy with survivors of trauma: To have our hearts broken.* New York: Routledge.

Almeida, R., Dolan-Del Vecchio, K., & Parker, L. (2007). *Transformative family therapy: Just families in a just society.* Boston: Allyn & Bacon.

Beneke, T. (1997). *Proving manhood: Reflections of men and sexism.* Berkley: University of California Press.

Dickerson, V. (2013). Patriarchy, power, and privilege: A narrative/poststructural view of work with couples. *Family Process, 52,* 102–114. doi:10.1111/famp.12018

Freire, P. (1970). *Pedagogy of the oppressed.* New York: Continuum.

Harvey, D. (2001). *Spaces of capital.* New York: Routledge.

Hooks, B. (2000). *Feminist theory: From margin to center.* Cambridge: South End Press.

Knudson-Martin, C. (2013). Why power matters: Creating a foundation of mutual support in couple relationships. *Family Process, 52*(1), 5–18. doi:10.1111/famp.12011

Lerner, G. (1986). *The creation of patriarchy.* Oxford: Oxford University Press.

Morely, C., & MacFarlane, S. (2012). The nexus between feminism and postmodernism: Still a central concern for critical social work. *British Journal of Social Work, 42*(4), 687–705.

Pease, B. (2000). Beyond the father wound: Memory-work and the deconstruction of the father-son relationship. *Australian & New Zealand Journal of Family Therapy, 21*(1), 9–15.

Pleck, J. (2014). Understanding patriarchy and men's power. *National organization for men against sexism.* http://www.nomas.ord/node/176. Accessed 29 July 2014.

Stanistreet, D., Bambra, C., & Scott-Samuel, A. (2005). Is patriarchy the source of men's higher mortality? *Journal of Epidemial Community Health, 59,* 873–876.

Walby, S. (1990). *Theorizing patriarchy.* Oxford: Basil Blackwell.

World Health Organization (2014). http://www.who.int/mental_health/prevention/genderwomen/en/. Accessed Sept 2014.

Chapter 4
Race and Family Therapy

There is no road toward racial equity that does not start with or lead to dismantling white privilege. I have my grandmother's cedar trunk at the end of my bed. The contents of the trunk were handed down from mother to daughter for eight generations of my mother's family. It is my turn now to keep the trunk and protect its contents. My mother's family has a long history in the USA, and while my grandmother was severely disabled and financially destitute, her ancestors were generally well educated and established. From time to time I open the trunk and take out intricate fabrics that were hand sewn in the early 1800s. I glance at my wall toward a Victorian crazy quilt bearing the name "Dixie" and the year 1885. I have always been proud of these treasures that represent female creativity and expression. Over time, however, I began to wonder how women in these eras were able to spend time completing arduous detailed embroidery. Who were they? Where and how did they live? From where did the name "Dixie" come? I remembered asking my mother and grandmother if our family ever "had slaves." They both answered "yes, but we were different. We were good to them." That was enough to ease my mind as a child.

I recently decided to look further; to try to re-member, re-connect to a past that has been cut off and distanced from our family legacy. I found census data in my ancestor's name along with descriptions of people by skin tone, gender, height, and weight without names. It is now less possible to forget. This legacy also belongs in the trunk as the means by which the contents were created; as an important part of family her-story to be passed to my granddaughter along with knowledge of my ancestor's attempts to protect this way of life in the Civil War (Dixie was named shortly after the war ended).

In this chapter I examine the meaning and impact of race in societal systems, family life, and therapeutic relationships through critical race theory (CRT) and critical decolonizing frameworks. CRT is contextually situated in the USA and can inform race relationships in at least some Western democracies with shared histories in which race is similarly constructed. The story of race in the USA and the world is, however, much more complex requiring an understanding of global colonial agendas to contextually situate race in any current context. Decolonizing theory expands

© American Family Therapy Academy 2015
T. McDowell, *Applying Critical Social Theories to Family Therapy Practice*,
AFTA SpringerBriefs in Family Therapy, DOI 10.1007/978-3-319-15633-0_4

the conversation to a global level. I explore white privilege within this framework. I then discuss multiracial families as a special topic followed by a case study and implications for the practice of family therapy.

Critical Race Theory

CRT emerged in the 1980s (Bell 1980; Bemal 2002; Delgado and Stefancic 2012) as a post-US civil rights legal discourse that challenges ongoing institutionalized racism. CRT has since been applied to other professional fields, including family therapy (McDowell 2004; McDowell and Jeris 2004). While there are no agreed upon tenets, critical race theorists share a commitment to social justice and racial equity. They generally agree that (1) racism and white privilege are systemic and institutionalized, thereby a normal part of everyday life; (2) race is a social construction with real material consequences; (3) race is one aspect of more complex multiple intersecting identities; (4) interdisciplinary approaches are essential to promoting equity; and (5) amplifying marginalized voices is important in challenging racism.

There is a good fit between CRT and family therapy. The feminist and critical multicultural critiques of family therapy resonate with CRT by drawing attention to systems of power, privilege, and oppression that routinely affect daily life. Family therapists have become increasingly aware of the impact of intersecting social identities, e.g., race, class, gender, sexual orientation, abilities. The social constructionist movement has shifted the practice of family therapy in a number of directions. Integrating social constructionist with critical frameworks recognizes the power dynamics related to how knowledge is constructed and the material consequences of these social constructions. Finally there is a growing emphasis in family therapy on witnessing the stories of those oppressed by dominant discourses and systems of oppression (McDowell and Jeris 2004).

Racism is Systemic

Critical race theorists acknowledge that social relationships in both historic and contemporary US society are organized around race (Ladson-Billings and Tate 1995). Race relationships systematically privilege whites over people of color. Differential privilege serves to maintain social class privilege (e.g., access to recourses, networks for seeking employment, comfort and safety of living arrangements). There is a plethora of historical examples of institutionalized racism: removing native children from their homes, Jim Crow laws, and Japanese internment are ready examples that occurred in recent US history. While laws and at least some social policies have changed in favor of racial equity, deeply entrenched systems of white legacy and privilege continue.

Race as a Social Construction

Race is now widely understood as a social construction. If race is socially constructed, then it is not real, leading many white families to teach their children to be colorblind. I am thinking of the first racial dialogue group I co-facilitated at a university family therapy clinic. We were working on how to bring up race in sessions. We were concerned that a white client was not connecting well with two therapists of color. The therapists decided to explore this by talking openly to the client about race and nation of origin differences. When they asked, "What is it like for you to work with us as African American and Indian therapists?" the client looked terrified quickly replying "Oh! I didn't notice!" This liberal approach is well-meaning, but denies the power and real material consequences of social constructs. This can make it difficult for families to work out racial problems. For example, I worked with a couple in which one partner was suffering racism at work on a daily basis. His white partner prided herself on not being racist, yet continually dismissed his complaints, stating things like "he is really sensitive about being Latino. I keep telling him it doesn't matter. We are all the same."

Interconnecting Identities

Multiple systems of privilege and oppression overlap and intersect to influence an individual's social standing in a given context. Race, gender, sexual orientation, social class, abilities, nation of origin, religion, ethnicity, looks, and personal attributes relative to specific contexts all make a difference and should be explored as contributing to relative privilege and oppression. It is not possible to analyze social dynamics without (1) understanding how these social identifiers intersect and (2) the multiple embedded global, historical, economic, social, political, and local contexts in which these identities have meaning. I am reminded of two supervisees with whom I worked. One was a white South African and the other was Indian. Their peers and clients responded to them quite differently often complimenting the South African on his accent, but asking the Indian if and when he "had to go back."

Interdisciplinary Approaches

Analysis of multiple systems is necessary to analyze the impact of the social location on individuals and families. This type of knowledge requires us to go beyond the field of family therapy and bring back knowledge from other disciplines such as anthropology, women's studies, law, political science, sociology, economics, education, and ethnic studies. In fact, maintaining an open system in which new knowledge can be brought in and adapted to promote mental and relational well-being is one of the hallmarks of family therapy (e.g., systems theory, postmodern philosophies).

Amplifying Marginalized Voices

Finally, there has been a trend in family therapy research to amplify marginalized voices (McDowell and Fang 2007). This is congruent with an emphasis on witnessing individual and family stories in therapy. Examples include families disclosing secrets to each other, therapists helping families listen to disempowered members, and co-constructing alternatives to problem-saturated narratives. The hope and expectation is that amplifying voices will make a difference, will influence power dynamics. Examples on a broad social level include multiracial, intersex, and transgender identity movements. As members of these groups share their experience, public opinion shifts with the hope that change in social policy will follow. In therapy, we often expect that once family members understand each other's thoughts, feelings, and experiences, they will empathize and allow themselves to be influenced. Sometimes this happens and sometimes it does not.

Race and the Colonial Agenda

Critical decolonizing theory sheds light on processes of colonization in contemporary society. Goals include reclaiming indigenous beliefs, values and practices; supporting cultural equity; and prioritizing pluriversal versus universal frameworks. Decolonizing frameworks also point to what is ambivalent, changing, and newly created as a result of colonial dynamics. I am reminded of a number of Native American clients. Shakers had established a missionary church years before and had become well established in their very rural Northwest community. Client after client reported problems based on the church's opposition to native tradition. For example, one client had dreams that foretold future events but did not dare tell the Shaker religious community. Another struggled with a difficult decision based on not being allowed to invite a respected elder to a Shaker wedding because the elder was a practicing shaman. These clients were able to hold the tensions inherent in maintaining traditional ways of knowing and doing while being members of the Shaker church. They lived in a pluriversal world. The church did not, demanding universal ideological dominance.

Colonizing includes dominating the resources, human labor, and trade markets of colonial territories and peoples. Control is secured through rhetoric that claims spiritual, intellectual, and other forms of superiority of the colonizer. The ethnocentric belief that the morals, values, and cultural practices of the colonizer are superior to those of the colonized helps justify domination. For example, my grandfather was a principal at an Indian school in New Mexico during the 1930s. Children were taken from their families on the reservation and placed in dorms. They were not allowed to speak their native language, wear native clothing, or practice native ceremonies. The boys had their traditional long hair cut. One of the stories I remember being told was about my grandfather's cruelty to a Native woman who cleaned his home. She had responded by threatening him—describing herself as a witch. What I remember most about the story is that it was meant to be funny; that it was not only a ridiculous, uncivilized notion but that she was foolish to believe she had any power.

Those of European descent colonized and continue to colonize in the USA. The cultural values, practices, language, traditions, and beliefs of colonizers are centered, marginalizing and disenfranchising all others. This is highly impacting in the practice of family therapy. Consider the dreamer I mentioned above. Having been trained in the Diagnostic and Statistical Manual of Mental Disorders (DSM), I found myself questioning whether or not reports of dreaming the future were real. Should I be diagnosing and referring someone with delusions? I clearly remember struggling with this and decided to believe the reports as actually occurring within a cultural context outside of my own. I thought, "What would my colleagues think if they knew I believe this client? What would this client think of my doubt?"

Whiteness as Property

The social construction of race and the myth of racial superiority promoted by most recent colonizers continues to privilege whiteness as valuable inheritance that affords its owners with both lateral (extended family) and vertical (family of origin and family of procreation) group privilege (Harris 1993). When I say "my white privilege" I also protect it as property—something I own. Ironically, we often say "you need to own your privileges" when emphasizing accountability. Harris (1993) argued that there is a connection between race and citizenship via the legal issue of property. She pointed to the fact that the USA is a nation built on property rights. The nation's founders recognized only white men as owners of property and as fully enfranchised members of society. African Americans were not only excluded from civil rights because they were neither white nor owned land, but they were in fact treated as property. In reference to a story she told about her own light-skinned African American grandmother passing as white in order to work, Harris (1993) explained:

> In ways so embedded that it is rarely apparent, the set of assumptions, privileges, and benefits that accompany the status of being white have become a valuable asset that whites sought to protect and that those who passed sought to attain—by fraud if necessary. Whites have come to expect and rely on these benefits, and over time, these expectations have been affirmed, legitimized and protected by the law. (p. 3)

Harris argued the legal foundation for property as a right to the determination of rules of its use rather than simple possession—just as whiteness as property has allowed its collective owners to define the rules of US society. Like property, whiteness is inherited as a protected asset from generation to generation.

Special Topic: Multiracial Families

The number of multiracial families is one of the most rapidly growing demographics in the USA. The multiracial identity movement emerged out of the racial equity social movements of the mid-twentieth century. As barriers to cross-race intimate relationships decreased, a greater number of biracial and multiracial children were born. Family therapists in the USA must be able to help all families navigate the racialized social context in which we live. Understanding and being able to fluidly talk about the dynamics of race and racism, racial and multiracial identity development, and multiracial family identity are among necessary competencies (McDowell et al. 2005).

As with many structural social movements, the civil rights/racial equity movements rely heavily on group identity and solidarity. Proudly claiming one's marginalized identity is an essential starting place for social movements, which require group action and strategized resistance to unfair laws, social policies, and public practices. While multiracial families can be seen as evidence of successful restructuring of race relationships, multiracial identity can challenge the solidarity of these movements. Multiracial individuals and families frequently experience invalidation of their identities. Families are often not recognized as such and familial relationships questioned. For example, I worked with a multiracial child who had a white mother. At age eight, he could not figure out why teachers and peers at school repeatedly asked "Is that your mom?" The fact that so many people questioned their belonging as a family made him "wish my mother's skin matched mine."

Those who identify as multiracial are often placed in forced choice situations; are you with us—one of us—or not? They are often assigned an identity based on visible phenotype alone, torn in their loyalties to more than one group. They may experience themselves as not belonging anywhere. I am reminded of many biracial children with whom I have worked who report that they do not feel like they fit in either extended family; white grandmothers favoring white cousins; family of color seeing them as only partially belonging.

Root (1996) proposed that there are multiple choices for multiracial identity including accepting the racial identity assigned by society, identifying with a single racial group, identify with more than one group, or identify as multiracial as an identity in and of itself. Multiracial families are often seen and see themselves as having multiracial members, but fail to recognize their family identity as multiracial (McDowell et. al. 2005). Multiracial families have unique needs relative to negotiating race. For example white parents often do not know how to help children of color resist racism. Partners may face rejection from families of origin for marrying outside their race. White partners often underestimate and fail to validate the daily racism their significant other's experience. Multiracial families are likely to have to learn to navigate what is for them new racial terrain of extended families, school and other institutional systems, and community relations.

Case Example

Louise and Martin were in their sixties when they agreed to adopt their two grand-daughters, ages 3 and 5. One of their children had become addicted to heroin, leaving her two children in need of a stable home. Louise and Martin courageously stepped up to the challenge of starting family life again from the beginning. Louise and Martin were white, living in a small white town in the Midwest, with all white family and friends. The granddaughters were biracial. The family came to therapy because Louise and Martin were concerned about the 5-year-old's self-esteem. She had begun asking about her parents, questioning looking different from her grand-parents and friends, and was having trouble with acting out behavior in kindergarten.

One of the first things the therapist noticed was how often the grandparents referred to the girls as "beautiful." Their answers to racial questions were typical of well-meaning white families: "we are all the same on the inside," "you are just as important as anyone else," and so on. It was clear that the girls were well loved in this family but the subtext of being reassured that they were "just as good as" reflected fear the girls would think they were "less than."

The therapist was able to take some important steps with this family. She was able to talk openly about race first to the grandparents and then within the nuclear and extended family. The family slowly shifted into recognizing themselves as a biracial family, not a family with biracial children. This allowed the grandparents and willing extended family members to explore what they needed to learn about race and racism to advocate for the children at school and help the children resist racism. The therapist opened the door to pursuing a relationship with the children's African American grandparents, which allowed the girls to have opportunities to explore their racial identity and two cultures more fully. This also offered Louise and Martin much needed support in caring for the children as well as necessary exposure to help them continue to develop racial awareness.

Implications for Practice

CRT opens many possibilities for understanding racial dynamics and talking about race in therapy. Following are three core considerations, including having critical conversations about race, exploring strategies for resisting racism, and building interest convergence toward racial equity.

Critical Conversations About Race

The ability to fluently talk about race and facilitate meaningful conversations about the impact of race is basic to the practice of family therapy. We are experts at getting people to talk to us, and each other, about what is silenced and socially avoided. Talking about race requires us to have a good working knowledge of race, to be able to assess each client's racial awareness and attitudes, and to skillfully manage conversations across racial divides. Critical conversations (Korin 1994) based on Freire's (1970) conscientization framework provide a structure for raising racial awareness (see McDowell, Chap. 7, this volume). Critical conversations include asking problem-posing questions (e.g., "What do you notice about...."), reflection (e.g., "Why do you think that is...."), and considering action (e.g., "What might you do....").

Strategies for Resisting Racism

In a small exploratory study, family therapy trainees of color shared their strategies for coping with racism in their educational programs and how they made decisions regarding speaking up when experiencing racism (McDowell 2004). Strategies for resistance included withdrawing, trying to understand and navigate power dynamics, yielding to get through racist situations, and speaking out. When asked about the decision to speak out, participants indicated there were three relevant questions: (1) How likely is it that I will be believed, i.e., will the racism be acknowledged? (2) What is the likelihood of change, i.e., will it do any good? And (3) What are the potential consequences, i.e., will I be in a worse situation if I say something?

This framework is useful when helping clients determine what to do about the racism in their lives. Therapists are often in a position of helping clients strategize against oppression. Understanding that there are multiple legitimate responses to oppression is important, particularly for therapists who have had the privilege in their lives to speak out without suffering serious consequences. Many of us have been taught that speaking out is the only legitimate or empowered stance to take and fail to recognize the vastly different consequences of overt action depending on the context and one's interconnected social location. I am thinking about a woman from South America who was continually passed over for promotion even though she was highly competent. As we worked together it became clear that she was experiencing discrimination based on her nation-of-origin, accent, skin tone, and gender. This was the first step—making sense of what was going on. She could then work on strategies. Should she yield on smaller issues? Should she leave the job? Stay silent? If she were to go to human resources, would she be believed? What consequences might she suffer? Would anything change?

Interest Convergence

Derrick Bell (1980) pointed to civil rights movements in the USA to argue that changes in law and social policy do not occur until those in power see change as in their own best interest. In other words, change is most likely when the interests of those in power and those struggling in resistance converge. Therapists must be able to connect with those in power and find convergence of goals, wants, and needs to support equity when there are social, community, and family imbalances in power. I am thinking about a white family in which the father of a grown daughter rejected her marriage to a man of color, cutting off any contact with his son-in-law. The therapist had to help this father understand how his racism affected his daughter and his relationship with her. Did he want to be connected to his daughter? To spend time with future grandchildren? To be included in family holidays? Once he recognized the price he was paying, the therapist began to help him rethink and consider breaking an intergenerational legacy of racism. Paulo Freire (1970) argued that liberation benefits the oppressed and the oppressors. While racism benefits whites socially and economically, it harms all of us psychologically, spiritually, and relationally.

References

Bell, D. (1980). Brown v board of education and the interest-convergence dilemma. *Harvard Law Review, 93*(3), 518–533.

Bemal, D. (2002). Critical race theory: Latino critical theory, and critical raced-gendered epistemologies: Recognizing students of color as holders and creators of knowledge. *Qualitative Inquiry, 8*(1), 105–125.

Delgado, R., & Stefancic, J. (2012). *Critical race theory: An introduction* (2nd ed). New York: New York University Press.

Freire, P. (1970). *Pedagogy of the oppressed*. New York: Continuum.

Harris, C. (1993). Whiteness as property. *Harvard law Review, 106,* 1707–1791.

Korin, E. C. (1994). Social inequalities and therapeutic relationships: Applying Freire's ideas to clinical practice. *Journal of Feminist Family Therapy, 5*(3/4), 75–98.

Ladson-Billings, G., & Tate, W. (1995). Toward a critical race theory of education. *Teachers College Record, 97*(1), 47–68.

McDowell, T. (2004). Exploring the racial experiences of graduate trainees: A critical race theory perspective. *The American Journal of Family Therapy, 32*(4), 305–324.

McDowell, T., & Jeris, L. (2004). Talking about race using critical race theory: Recent trends in the journal of marital and family therapy. *Journal of Marital and Family Therapy, 30*(1), 81–94.

McDowell, T., & Fang, S. (2007). Feminist informed critical multiculturalism: Considerations for family research. *Journal of Family Issues, 28*(4), 549–566.

McDowell, T., Dashiell, W., Holland, C., Ingoglia, L., Serizawa, T., & Stevens, C. (2005). Raising multiracial awareness in family therapy through critical conversations. *Journal of Marital and Family Therapy, 31*(4), 399–411.

Root, M. P. P. (1996). *The multiracial experience: Racial borders as the new frontier*. Thousand Oaks: Sage.

Chapter 5
Queer Theory in the Practice of Family Therapy

Recently my 7-year-old grandchild said, "Grandma, maybe I will grow up to be a boy or maybe I will grow up to be a girl…I might marry a boy or I might marry a girl." I told my grandchild that there were lots of choices and that she did not even have to decide. We talked about how sometimes friends and teachers want you to be one thing or another. I also told her that when I was little sometimes I felt more like a girl and sometimes I felt more like a boy, but most of the time I just felt like me and that it has worked out ok. More and more young people are challenging binaries of sex, gender, and sexual orientation. They are demanding the freedom to express themselves as they choose.

In this chapter I explore the potential impact of queer theory on the construction of sex, gender, and sexual orientation in the practice of couple and family therapy. Queer theory provides a framework for questioning and resisting binary systems to promote flexibility in individual and relational identities (Carroll et al. 2002). I offer cisgenderism as a special topic, followed by a case example and implications of queer theory for the practice of family therapy.

Queer Theory

Queer theory challenges categorized identities, including what is commonly referred to as sex, gender, and sexual orientation (Wilchins 2004). It draws from multiple disciplines including political science, critical social theory, post-structural theory, women's studies, and gay and lesbian studies (Butler 1990, 2004; Marinucci 2010; Aydemir 2011). Feminist theory, gay and lesbian studies, and queer theory share the goal of decentering what is assumed "normal and natural" to transform unequal social relations. Knowledge about human experience is viewed as meaningful within context and its production affected by power rather than being universal, objective, and generalizable. Whereas all of these theories problematize categories and binaries, queer theory aims to dismantle and dispose of the use of categories all

© American Family Therapy Academy 2015
T. McDowell, *Applying Critical Social Theories to Family Therapy Practice,*
AFTA SpringerBriefs in Family Therapy, DOI 10.1007/978-3-319-15633-0_5

together (Butler 1990, 2004; Hudak and Giammattei 2010). According to McDowell, Emerick, and Garcia (2014):

> Queer theory is inclusive by nature of its blurring the middle and fringing the center. In effect, there can be no exclusion when the center no longer exists. Queer theory teases one with the possibility of something else, something other than what seems to be there, something that may have been there all along. Most critical to conceptualizing queer theory is to erase all notions of dominant/oppressed, right/wrong, normal/abnormal, truth/untruth. (p. 102)

The Social Construction of Sex, Gender, and Sexual Orientation

In this section, I draw a critical eye toward how sex, gender, and sexual orientation are defined, and consider implications relative to how these concepts are constructed. Sex can be understood as an organizational category at a medical level that is also used to prescribe gender. We are assigned an identity of either male or female based on visible genitalia at birth. So important is the shape of our genitalia that sex is often imposed resulting in unnecessary or even harmful surgical procedures to increase congruency between assigned sex and genitalia (Lev 2004).

Gender is a social construct that determines and justifies as natural the division of roles and tasks as well as imbalances of power in both public and intimate relationships. The bifurcation of gender is foundational to social arrangements. For example rituals in most cultures prescribe what men and women are to do (e.g., heterosexual weddings). Some religions (e.g., Islam, Orthodox Judaism) separate men and women during worship. Division of household labor and parenting tasks are common examples.

Gender is often described as a continuum in contrast to the purportedly mutually exclusive categories of sex. This continuum places traditional, culturally defined masculine behaviors and attitudes at one end and traditional, culturally defined feminine behaviors and attitudes at the other. For example, providing comfort and emotional understanding has been most often associated with being feminine. Taking charge and being brave in the face of physical danger has most often been associated with being masculine. Many claim androgynous identities, choosing characteristics, behaviors, and attitudes from across the spectrum or continuum. This notion of continuum increases flexibility but maintains a bipolar definition of gender. Gender must continually be expressed, or performed, to maintain the social meaning of femininity and masculinity. How gender is performed may or may not be congruent with what is socially expected or accepted of us based on our assigned sex or fit our own gender identity (Butler 1990, 2004).

Sexual orientation refers to physical and/or emotional attraction to members of the same sex, different sex, or both/all sexes. Categorizing sex, gender, and sexual orientation "preserves and protects a binary understanding of center versus another, normal versus different, natural versus unnatural, and ultimately identity versus deviance" (McDowell et al. 2014, p. 102).

Holding Tensions

McDowell et al. (2014) argued that working across feminist and queer frameworks to encourage just relationships requires the ability to balance opposing ideas. As family therapists, we are accustomed to holding multiple realities of family members at the same time, in the same space. Working toward identity-based equity while dismantling rigid dichotomies of sex, gender, and sexual orientation requires us to hold the tensions between and among epistemological paradigms that are commonly defined as mutually exclusive. Sex, gender, and sexual orientation are not the only categories of identity for which this is relevant. For example, race is socially constructed—there is no biological basis for categorical distinctions. The goal of dismantling the false ideology of race is clearly a goal in anti-racist work. Not referring to race while it holds widespread meaning and real material consequences, however, maintains inequities organized and justified through social construction of race as an identity. In other words, we cannot jump to what we think should be without acknowledging and working to change what is.

It is also helpful to recognize that most of us hold identity tensions about ourselves. For example, our private thoughts about our sex, gender, or sexual orientation often do not match our relational or public performance of these constructs. To various degrees we live with multiple consciousness around sex, gender, and sexual orientation (McDowell et al. 2014). For example, when I was in my 20s I wore men's clothing most of the time, but felt very female in a heterosexual relationship with a highly masculine partner. I was attracted to men and satisfied with a single male partner. My multiple consciousness included identifying physically as a female, but never secure as a tall woman who did not fit what I believed to be an ideal female physicality; identifying as a woman who felt more masculine than I imagined other women feeling. The lived experience and consequences of these tensions are unevenly distributed among us depending on the congruence between how we know ourselves and what is expected of us in particular contexts.

Special Topic: Cisgenderism

Cisgender refers to individuals who self-identify as a gender that matches the sex that was assigned to them at birth. While sex assignment and gender identity are not the same thing, these are often conflated in our everyday understanding of gender identity. Cisgenderism is an ideology that "others" those whose gender identity does not align with assigned sex at birth. Cisgenderism is discrimination against those who perform and/or experience gender in ways that do not culturally align with the sex they were assigned at birth. Everyday examples of institutionalized cisgenderism include forms and language that force choice between male and female, male–female assigned bathrooms, prison assignment based on genitalia, and gender dysphoria as a diagnosis in the DSM V. Informal cisgenderism includes bullying, beating, and excluding those who cross the socially prescribed gender line. Cisgenderism perpetuates the ideology that experiencing and performing one's gender in ways that are socially congruent with what others assign as your sex is preferable and more highly valued than what is termed in contrast as transgender identities. To the degree we experience and are seen by others to fit into our assigned gender, we can be said to hold cisgender privilege. This includes those of us who can pass as along the spectrum of our assigned sex through our gender expression, even if we do not experience gender–sex congruence.

I want to note here the importance of cisgenderism to the maintenance of male privilege and patriarchy. Patriarchy is based on systematic divisions of the distinct and mutually exclusive categories of male and female. This is institutionalized across most societies prescribing gendered power dynamics within religion, politics, economics, and family life. Boys and men are often quickly ridiculed and corrected at the first sign of nonconformance with how their assigned sex is to be gendered (Kimmel 2008). Assigned females who perform masculine identities are also scorned in a system that reserves male behavior and male privilege for those with male genitalia. Those with the most to lose fear that blurring or getting rid of the gender lines will inevitably dismantle gender-based systems of privilege, causing a fall in systems of patriarchy. I also want to point to Ansara and Hegarty's (2012) critique of the idea and use of the term cisgender as itself oppressive—yet one more way to oppress through creating a category which by its very nature defines those within and those not within its definition.

Case Example

After 5 years of trying to solve their problems on their own, Polly and David came into therapy to talk about their sex life. Polly and David identified as white, middle-class, heterosexual, US born, and nonreligious. Both Polly and David worked in computer technology and met in college. When they graduated, they were able to find jobs in the same company. Polly moved up quickly and was now in a higher administrative position than David. While David took some ribbing from coworkers about his wife being the boss, he voiced his pride in Polly's achievements and his relief that she made such a good income. The problem was that while Polly and David were both interested in sex, Polly often found it difficult to reach orgasm. The sexual ritual they enacted included David showering and putting on aftershave, Polly dressing in something "seductive," spending time together relaxing and stroking one another, and then moving on to genital stimulation, oral sex, and then vaginal intercourse. They were making all the right moves, so why the problem?

As the therapist talked with the couple about their work and lives together, she questioned Polly's ability to move up in a male-dominated field. Polly talked about her comfort and ability to demonstrate traditionally male exclusive work traits—she put in long hours, kept a competitive eye on her peers, focused on the bottom line, and articulated her ideas well in the presence of those in power. Polly did not barter female sexuality for male favor—she dressed and presented herself with an eye toward androgyny. David, on the other hand, preferred being one of the guys at work, displaying more cooperation than competition, keeping work and leisure time in balance, and keeping out of the way of top executives. He was free to dress in masculine business casual. While David was routinely invited to male-only conversations about female coworkers, Polly was isolated from both all-male and all-female groups.

Polly described herself as having been a "tomboy" from the time she was very young. She embraced this identity and enjoyed having both male and female friends. David dabbled in sports, liked technology, and mostly hung out with other boys. Polly and David were attracted to each other because of similar interests and senses of humor, physical attraction, and the potential for an equal, collaborative partnership. Yet sexually, Polly felt self-conscious and David felt responsible for ensuring Polly was sexually satisfied.

The therapist explored the impact of their sexual fantasies, sexual identities, and gender identities on their performance of sex. David understood his role as a man as one of sexual performance with the ultimate test being his ability to cause Polly to have an orgasm. Polly believed that in the female role, she should be the object of desire to be acted upon. Polly had been socialized that as a female, her role was to be attractive to males and this pervaded her thoughts during sex. These gender roles did not fit their gendered identities. Polly's sexual fantasies included being the pursuer, visualizing sexualized male and female bodies, and imagining her own body in more masculine than feminine form. When having sex with David, she playacted an inauthentic sexual script for the fear of not fitting with what she assumed were his interests and desires. David was also not authentic as he playacted a more traditional masculine role than the way he gendered himself elsewhere in their lives.

Polly deeply experienced herself as a gender variant—not fitting into a gender binary. She managed this balance in most aspects of her life, passing on the outside as more feminine than she identified on the inside. The therapist facilitated difficult socially prohibited conversations with Polly and David in ways that raised their critical consciousness of the social construction of gender. Eventually, Polly and David liberated themselves from internal dialogues about sexual scripts (internalized cisgenderism). Polly was able to take a more active role in her own satisfaction, indulge in a wider variety of fantasy, and worry less about David's male gaze on her as a female. David was able to relax and enjoy sex with less focus on performance and more of the playful collaboration he enjoyed in the rest of his life.

Implications for Practice

Queer theory can be liberating for all of us. It allows us to open space for clients (and ourselves) to imagine previously unmapped landscapes of attraction, sexual expression, and gender (non)performance. Queer theory can be meaningfully applied to all aspects of our gendered relationships and identities. The case example described above demonstrates these points specifically in sex therapy. According

1. Ask clients for their preferred use of pronoun before addressing as "she/he/they." Don't assume sexual orientation or partner affiliation.

2. Insist on gender-neutral bathrooms and the use of gender-neutral forms at your agency/practice. When necessary for reporting requirements, use open-ended requests for sex, gender and sexual orientation.

3. Allow children, adolescents and adults to explore sex, gender, and sexual orientation without pressing for decisions or implying the need to categorize.

4. Help parents accept children who express sex, gender and sexual orientation in ways that the family may not have expected. Avoid labeling.

5. Raise critical consciousness in therapy around the social construction of sex, gender, and sexual orientation and challenge inequity based on these constructions (see McDowell, Chapter 7, this volume).

6. Refer clients to identity and human rights organizations for education and support, e.g., the Intersex Society of North America (http://www.isna.org); National Center for Transgender Equality (http://transequality.org/); American Civil Liberties Union (www.aclu.org), World Health Organization (http://www.who.int), the Universal Declaration of Human Rights (http://www.un.org/en/documents/udhr/).

7. Become familiar with organizations such as those listed above, learn as much as possible about promoting equity across sex, gender and sexual orientation, and consider the impact of human rights in the practice of family therapy (McDowell, Libal& Brown, 2012).

8. Learn to hold the tension of sex, gender, and sexual orientation as categories of difference that need to be addressed to support relational equity while viewing them as social constructions of difference. This includes listening carefully to how clients think about sex, gender and sexual orientation.

9. Consider sex, gender, and sexual orientation as within a complex matrix of identities that include race, social class, religion, nation of origin, age, abilities, and ethnicity as meaningful within specific contexts.

10. Do your own work relative to sex, gender identity, and sexual orientation, including beliefs, assumptions, and attitudes that impact your work.

Fig. 5.1 Ten things therapists can do from a queer perspective

to Iasenza (2010) queer theory contributes to the practice of sex therapy in several important ways that can be applied more generally:

> First, it [queer theory] reminds us of the potential fluidity and multidimensionality of same and other sex/gender experience in all people. Such a therapeutic conceptual frame creates safe space for clients to (re)imagine themselves in whatever inclusive or expansive ways they need. Second, it embodies the confounding nature of sexuality in general with its incongruities and paradoxes in sexual behaviors, attractions, thoughts, feelings, fantasies, and sensations. Thirdly, it normalizes our awkwardness as we challenge our own cherished frames about sexuality and gender in clinical practice. (p. 292)

As therapists we need to reflect on the understanding of the complexities of gender and sexual orientation. I offer some practical suggestions in Fig. 5.1 for what we might do to reflect queer informed practice.

This chapter has centered on sex, gender, and sexual orientation without deeply engaging in intersections of race, class, nation of origin, religion, and other identifiers. This creates part-truths about sex, gender, and sexual orientation that are largely out of context. These complex matrixes need to be considered as a whole just as we are whole beings. In sum, I have argued that queer theory and other post-structural understandings of categorical differences can be useful in family therapy to fray the edges of identity markers liberating us from limiting dichotomies and categorical understandings of ourselves and others.

References

Ansara, Y.G., & Hegarty, P. (2012). Cisgenderism in psychology: Pathologising and misgendering children from 1999 to 2008. *Psychology & Sexuality, 3*(2), 137–160. doi:10.1080/08975353. 2013.849551.

Aydemir, M. (2011). *Indiscretions: At the intersection of queer and postcolonial theory.* Amsterdam: Rodopi.

Butler, J. (1990). *Gender trouble: Feminism and the subversion of identity.* New York: Routledge.

Butler, J. (2004). *Undoing gender.* New York: Routledge.

Carroll, L. C., Gilroy, P. J., & Ryan, J. (2002). Counseling transgendered, transsexual, and gender-variant clients. *Journal of Counseling and Development, 80,* 131–139. doi:10.1002/j.1556–6678.2002.tb00175

Hudak, J., & Giamattei, S. (2010). Doing family: Decentering heteronormativity on 'couple' and 'family' therapy. Winter monograph: American Family Therapy Academy. www.psychology-today.com/files/attachments/45260/hudak-and-giammattei-doing-family-12-09.pdf. Accessed 15 Dec 2014.

Iasenza, S. (2010). What is queer about sex? Expanding sexual frames in theory and practice. *Family Process, 49*(3), 291–308. doi:10.1111/j.1545–5300.2010.01324.x.

Kimmel, M. (2008). *Guyland: The perilous world where boys become men.* New York: Harper Perennial.

Lev, I.A. (2004). *Transgender emergence: Therapeutic guidelines for working with gender-variant people and their families.* Binghamton: The Haworth Clinical Practice Press.

Marinucci, M. (2010). *Feminism is queer: The intimate connection between queer and feminist theory.* New York: Palgrave Macmillan.

McDowell, T., Emerick, P. & Garcia, M. (2014). Queering family therapy education. *Journal of Feminist Family Therapy, 7*(2), 99–112. doi:10.1080/08952833.2014.893805

Wilchins, R. (2004). *Queer theory, gender theory: An instant primer.* Los Angeles: Alyson Publications.

Chapter 6
Pace, Place, and Just Practice

Family therapists rarely consider the impact of a family's geography—where they live, the safety and comfort of their environment, their ability to move from one place to another to seek resources, their level of privacy and control over the spaces they occupy—on their psychological, emotional and relational well-being. The choices families have regarding where and how to live are determined by many factors including economic resources, available family and community networks, social policy, and global politics. Think of a Hmong family that has left the mountains of Laos to escape persecution after the Vietnam War. Part of the family resides in a refugee camp in Thailand and another part of the family was evacuated to the USA. In agreeing to cooperate with US forces, Hmong families politically shifted from being marginalized to being at high risk for loss of life and liberty. This global political situation led to intergenerational disruption of extended families and major changes in the community's way of life. This would have a great deal to do with health and relational well-being of a Hmong family seeking therapy.

Power dynamics are interconnected across all levels of society, from global as exemplified above to local, within the most intimate territory of the home. For example, more powerful members of the family often set the emotional tone of shared space and dictate what will happen in that space. The sound of my father's footsteps coming up the stairs signaled an immediate change in the emotional climate and shift in family interactions. I would typically withdraw to my room and engage in quiet, solitary activities. If too late to retreat undetected, I would hold myself in a state of tension in the shared space until I could exit. The fact that our home included individual bedrooms into which one could withdraw was a reflection of privilege.

In this chapter, I introduce critical geography to the practice of family therapy focusing on the impact of space and place. I consider privacy, personal space, social interactions, and safety in community and social life. I then explore relationships between social class and mobility; race and segregation; and boundaries and resistance. I introduce what I am calling *family cartography* as a special topic and apply this technique to my own family and community of origin to exemplify how family

© American Family Therapy Academy 2015
T. McDowell, *Applying Critical Social Theories to Family Therapy Practice,*
AFTA SpringerBriefs in Family Therapy, DOI 10.1007/978-3-319-15633-0_6

therapists might use it to meaningfully explore the impact of space and place on ourselves and on those with whom we work.

Critical Geography

At first glance, critical geography may seem out of place in the field of family therapy. Typically we are more interested in time than space. Genograms, life maps, family histories, and life stories rely heavily on the dimension of time. Many techniques that pay attention to space, such as sculpts and structural maps, only highlight space within the emotional/relational field of the family. It is typical to ask about family her/history, track a problem/solution over time, or draw patterns of interaction. But what about space? What might family therapists do differently if space were considered more equally alongside time? In this section, I rely heavily on the work of Edward Soja (2010) and his critical postmodern concept of spatiality. I offer an overview of a number of topics raised in critical geography that highlight space as a social justice issue and then apply these ideas to the politics of space within families and communities.

Critical geographers draw from a variety of approaches including feminism, critical race theory, environmental justice, postmodernism, social constructionism, and Marxist traditions to understand and challenge the impact of power in the dynamics of space and place. Critical geography is concerned with social and spatial justice, often pointing to the geographical consequences of misuse of power evidenced by actions such as relegation of indigenous peoples to reservations; the impact of capitalist production on inner city conditions; displacement of low status communities through gentrification; and pollution of lands inhabited by members of marginalized communities. Critical geography can inform our understanding of the politics of space within families and of families within communities.

Space

Space refers to the actual physical environment, e.g., the items in the environment, their shape and size, and the distance between them. This includes the natural environment and what humans physically and socially construct (e.g., educational institutions, medical care facilities, homes, parks, nuclear power plants, shopping malls, and employment sites). Soja (2010) argued that time, space, and social interactions are all primary in the construction of our identities and the material realities of our lives. In-home family therapists have long been aware of the impact of space and place on families, recognizing the value of meeting families in their home environment. How space is organized and used, who has access to which spaces, and the concept of private versus public property are all related to spatial justice. Therapists commonly ask couples to take a walk together or go on a family outing, but which clients can safely do this and enjoy the experience without trepidation? Parents are encouraged to set limits for teens going out at night. But how often do we consider what is reasonable based on the context in which the family lives?

The greater access we have to resources (e.g., education, clean water and air, medical services, and employment) the more likely we are to parlay that access into greater advantage. Those with similar capital tend to share social space via neighborhoods, schools, parks, and workplaces. Bourdieu (1986) argued that it is within social space—or habitus—that we learn, internalize, and embody shared ways of thinking and doing, values, and beliefs. Space is, therefore, essential in understanding worldview, culture, and class. Consider what it might mean to include an analysis of space when constructing a genogram. For example, a family story about a grandfather disposing of newborn puppies takes on a different meaning within the physical context of the Great Depression—when there was not enough food or resources to meet basic needs, no resources for unwanted animals. Shared beliefs about hard work and frugality are common among those who lived through that time, in that space. In fact like time, space affects everything and everything is affected by space. According to Soja (2010):

> Viewed from above, every place on earth is blanketed with thick layers of macrospatial organization arising not just from administrative convenience but also from the imposition of political power, cultural domination, and social control over individuals, groups, and the places they inhabit. (p. 540)

Families are obviously affected by space. Where we live, what resources we can access within our neighborhoods, the quality of the environment to which we are exposed, and our homes are just a few examples of the very real impact of space. Families with economic means are often able to secure housing that is psychologically uplifting, has enough room for expression of individual needs, is owned creating a sense of family agency and independence, and is situated in safe, quiet neighborhoods. By contrast, those living on low income often share small spaces between family members, have no insulation against the sound of streets and neighbors, are vulnerable to the intrusion of landlords, have limited choice about when and where they can go outside due to safety concerns, and suffer the ill effects of disproportionately high pollution. The high stress associated with living in these spaces is evidenced by higher rates of mental illness, psychiatric hospitalization, and schizophrenia (Hudson 2012), as well as elevated poor health and high mortality rates (Fitzpatrick and MaGlory 2000). For example, I have met with many families who worked in cedar shake mills in the rural northwest USA. While they had clean air and water as well as a good working wage, they were poorly insulated against health hazards. It was not uncommon for accidents to leave uninsured workers disabled with few recourses for reemployment. The effect on families was devastating as tension, stress, and conflict increased. In therapy, we battled a sense of hopelessness that threatened these families who felt place bound without adequate resources. Similar dynamics occur in urban areas. Fitzpatrick and MaGlory (2011) argued that in the inner city, four groups are particularly vulnerable relative to physical and mental health: the poor, the homeless, the youth, and the elders. These groups share "limited action spaces" (p. 152) as they rely heavily on their immediate surroundings, which are often woefully inadequate to meet basic needs and often expose them to violence, pollution, noise, and other stressors.

Space also refers to distance between people and their access to each other. The computer era has drastically changed spatial social arrangements, as we are now able to communicate instantly at any physical distance. This allows for compression of time and space (Harvey 2001), favoring and helping realize the expectation in technologically advanced settings that getting what we want and need should be frictionless. This time–space compression has increased the ease with which ideas can be shared impacting many arenas including collective resistance (e.g., the Arab Spring), kinship systems, and global capitalism. Through cyberspace, ideal material worlds are created that cannot realistically be attained by most, increasing expectation in the marketplace, which in turn fuels consumerism and capitalist profit (Einstein 1998). For example, many young families in India have moved to urban areas for well-paying high tech positions. They are physically separated from joint families. There is pressure to produce more and consume more, creating emotional and relational problems not previously prevalent.

Families are affected by the compression of time and space in negative and positive ways. Some negative effects include media pressure to consume increasing the need to work and the tension around money. Affairs, gambling, and pornography are more accessible online than in real time and space. Internet and video addictions have emerged as problems in need of family and therapeutic intervention (Hertlein and Ancheta 2014). Militarization of US culture is more easily delivered through movies and video games (Giroux 2014). On a more positive note, families are able to easily obtain knowledge that was once restricted to professional experts. Social networks combat isolation and increase access to support networks. Liberating ideas and groups are more available creating virtual communities that can encourage positive social change. Think of identity movements (e.g., intersex rights movement, transgender identity movement, and polyamory movement) and how what was once privately encased in shame is now more readily accessible, shedding light on the realities of lived experience and promoting acceptance of difference. These changes affect the practice of family therapy including the types of therapeutic interventions available, the types of problems we treat, and our ongoing deliberations regarding the effectiveness and ethics of online therapy.

Place

Place refers to a sense of being in a space. A sense of place is connected to meeting basic human needs of privacy, personal space, availability of social interactions, and safety. While expectations vary between cultures, these needs are fairly universal (Fitzpatrick and LaGory 2011). The old adage "there's no *place* like home" reflects the way we connect and feel about certain places—specific places hold meaning. The significance of place is easily illustrated by examples of willingness to fight to secure sacred grounds for one's religious group (e.g., Crimean War and Israeli–Palestinian Conflict). Similar places at different locations can hold meaning. Think of going to a mosque, temple, synagogue, church, or any important place for a religion to which you belong. Stepping in can capture a sense of belonging and security even when thousands of miles from home. Connection to the natural environment is also meaningful. For example, I grew up at the foot of the San Francisco Peaks in Arizona and 40 years later still feel most comfortable in geographical areas with tall trees and mountains. Within my worldview these physical environments are nurturing. Consider, however, the difference in choice, meaning, and impact for indigenous people living in the same area a 100 years earlier. The Dine (Navajos) were forced by the US soldiers to leave places where sacred spirits reside, including the Dook'ó'ooslííd (San Francisco Peaks), to relocate to a space without similar meaning via the Navajo Long Walk. The example of the Navajo Long Walk and many other colonizing efforts throughout history exemplify misuse of power over one group by another. This is related not only to place but to privacy, personal space, preferred social interactions, and safety. Considering each of these needs relative to families within the context of their homes, neighborhoods, and communities makes visible what is often invisible in the therapy room.

Privacy, Personal Space, Social Interactions, and Safety

Restriction of and forced movement, surveillance, bodily intrusion, and assault are all abuses of power within spaces we inhabit. Migration is often motivated by home no longer being safe, not having access to necessary resources to survive, losing the right to privacy, or personal space being eliminated/threatened. These situations are often created via one country or people attempting to colonize or overpower another. Movement can also be forced as in human trafficking, slavery, and internment. Removing indigenous peoples to reservations is inhumane on multiple levels, including not only distance from culturally and spiritually meaningful places, but the denial of privacy, personal space, customary social interactions, and safety through forced movement, physical assault, and surveillance. Once the US troops quashed Dine resistance through the use of lethal weaponry, remaining tribal members were lined up and marched at gunpoint from various places in Arizona and Western New Mexico to Ft. Sumner in Eastern New Mexico. Surveillance was constant and intrusive. Cultural and social interactions were interrupted. Those who could not keep up due to age, illness, or childbirth were shot and/or left behind (Tohe 2007). Additional examples of denial of privacy, personal space, and safety that occur routinely include rape, torture, stalking, and assault.

There are also everyday dynamics of power and space that are intended to protect. Keeping children from putting their heads out the car window or from running into the street protects them. Imprisonment of violent criminals protects society. Going beyond necessary surveillance is, however, a misuse of power and denies basic rights to privacy. Consider Sheriff Joe Arpaio's use of jail cams in Arizona.

Webcams were set up in numerous locations and broadcasted live stream to the public. Anyone could then view male and female prisoners sleeping, strapped in chairs for rule violations, being strip searched, or using the bathroom.

Surveillance is about watching or gazing. Those with more power often gaze upon those with less power. Consider the (heterosexual) male gaze on female sexuality; tourists from wealthy countries taking pictures of people in everyday activity in poor countries; and humans placing animals in cages to provide constant access to viewing. Gaze can also be demanded as happens in classrooms in which all participants are to have their eyes on the instructor. In all of these examples, it is the more powerful who determine the terms of gazing.

Public surveillance is increasingly entering private lives as exemplified by webcams that are now situated to survey individual actions on most city streets and in many private businesses. Level of intrusion and protection from intrusion are often class-based. The poor, particularly those on welfare in the USA, are routinely under government surveillance. This historically meant inspecting homes for eligibility and currently includes monitoring who is living in the household, scanning for activities that produce extra income, and accessing private health and employment records (Gilliom 2001). This is highly influential in therapy. Take for example a family that has been referred by the department of social services for child neglect. The family often views the therapist as an extension of the state's surveillance and is reluctant to be truthful for fear of the consequences. Meanwhile, the therapist reports back to the state that the family was noncooperative. The majority of welfare recipients are female head of households, which raises the question of government social control of women and children when patriarchs are absent from the family (see McDowell, Chap. 3, this Volume).

Those who are homeless worldwide often have no privacy, personal space, or way to defend safe space. They are subject to limited and often unwanted or distasteful social interactions. For example, I worked with a family in which a young child had been sexually abused by an adult in the home in which her mother was staying. Disclosure of the abuse meant yet another move for this homeless family. The child described the paper bag she carried with her from home to home. All of her belongings were in the bag. Her clothing was highly distressed and failed to cover the most intimate parts of her body. Moving in with another family friend meant once again being subject to a constant sense of not being safe, wanted, or at home. The rich are often securely tucked into safe communities and spaces where police protection is adequate. They have ample privacy in their homes, personal space in offices, cars and houses, and can access the types of social interactions they prefer.

Mobility

Mobility—including freedom of, and potential for, movement and therefore flexibility to better one's circumstances—is unevenly distributed based on class, race, gender, sexual orientation, language, and nation of origin. Mobility potential (Jensen 2011) is rarely identified as part of privilege matrixes, nor is lack of mobility potential recognized as compounding oppression. The greater our mobility potential the greater our ability to move from one place to another to engage in leisure, participate in higher education, maintain geographically distant family relationships, build support networks, take a better job, and/or access resources. It is not uncommon for mental health agencies that serve the poor to have strict policies about being late or missing appointments even though bus schedules, cost of transportation, length of time in transit, and difficulty getting multiple family members gathered to use public transportation are rarely considered when appointments are scheduled.

Occupational status associated with income frequently affects movement during work hours. For example, a business owner may stay within the same space each day, but has the power to choose when to get up from her desk, when to take a short nap, and when to leave and return to the office. She can approach her staff at any time interrupting their work and holding their attention as long as she deems necessary. On the other hand, her employees have far more limited mobility, often being required to stay at a desk, cash register or loading dock for set amounts of time, risking being fired should they enter and linger in their employer's private office or leave their posts for unscheduled breaks. Those in the Global South (including the Global South within all major cities) are more place-bound than those in the Global North. This makes it relatively simple to access labor in low resource countries and areas in the city and sell it as goods in high resource countries and city spaces.

Restriction and negotiation of movement and mobility is often a source of conflict in families. Children's mobility potential is tied to parent's mobility and parental restriction of mobility. Whether a child can play sports is likely influenced by a parent's ability to provide transportation. A child's breaking family rules may result in restriction of movement being imposed (e.g., refusing to provide the required ride to sports practice). Where families live and whose career is benefited or truncated based on this decision is a major equity issue faced by dual earner families. Young families often struggle over who gets time away from caring for children to pursue adult interests. These are just a few among many examples.

Segregation

Segregation is also a way to limit mobility of those with less power and resources for the benefit of those with more power and resources. According to Fitzpatrick and LaGory (2011), "segregation is a powerful spatial force protecting the status quo ... highly segregated groups find themselves isolated from the organizational structures and resources necessary to promote health and well-being" (p. 14). This may be highly formal and institutionalized. For example, after the US Civil War, Black Codes were adopted by states to regulate blacks and maintain white supremacy. These laws prevented freedom of movement of free blacks and limited them to low paying jobs. Vagrancy laws in Southern states allowed police to arrest blacks for loitering in public space and place them in involuntary servitude. After World Wars I/II, southern black migrants were recruited by northern industry as strikebreakers to interfere with white worker unions. Once established, unions then promoted racial segregation on the job and blocked blacks from white union ranks. African Americans were cut off from productive work and geographically constricted in what eventually became urban ghettos, becoming a disposable workforce as industry moved to suburban locations. Many states and cities adopted laws that prevented selling real estate to African Americans outside of specific locations. The practice of redlining refers to mapping areas where banks will not invest, public improvements are not made, and new business is discouraged. For example, in Chicago, African Americans were not allowed to purchase homes outside the once industrial section of the city where they were originally recruited to work. Once industries moved out of the area, there were no jobs and no way to leave. The resulting poverty and social degradation eventually became seen as a result of being black and poor rather than the result of unfettered capitalism and racial redlining. Now consider contemporary mental health services that reach out to families in these areas. What attitudes do family therapists carry with them about poverty, intergenerational poverty, race and poverty, about the relationship between poverty, race and mental health? Now imagine the empowering impact of using cultural circles (Almeida et al. 2007) to raise critical consciousness about race, segregation, poverty, and the prison industrial complex among youth and families living in these areas.

Boundaries, Borders, and Resistance

Boundaries have to do with limits and divisions—where we draw the line relative to personal boundaries, boundaries between countries, boundaries within and between families, and boundaries around identities (i.e., who we are and who we are not). Boundaries become particularly salient at their borders. Harding (2008) described borderlands as spaces of complexity and strain, where contention between groups is acted out. Borderlands are spaces where marginalization, exclusion, and oppression meet resistance. The border between the USA and Mexico is a prime example. The US pours significant tax dollars and human resources into defending the Southern border it took by force via the Mexican American War. The United States social policy forbids working without a visa, yet the US economy depends in part on an undocumented workforce. The toll of this border arrangement is heavily leveled on those from Mexico who live daily with the consequences of inhabiting these borderlands and crossing in resistance (Anzaldua 2007). Borderlands also refer to boundaries around identity groups. For example, Callis (2014) talked about the borderlands between heterosexual and homosexual binaries as inhabited by pan-sexual, bisexual, and queer identities. It is also in these borderlands that new ideas and practices emerge and space is made for things like living in multiple cultures, speaking more than one language, and identifying outside prescribed categories of gender and sexual orientation. The result is often a hybrid of cultural differences creating new ideas, religious, cultural and social practices, business opportunities, foods, clothing, and professions. This is an important concept in strength-based family therapy. For example, biracial clients often describe a sense of not fitting anywhere—living in the borderlands of racial identity. In therapy, we explore the strength and resilience that has resulted from continuously crossing cultural bor-ders, as well as the unique practices, attitudes, and ideas they have developed as a result. Working with transnational families is another good example. These families often traverse economic, political, and cultural borders in unique ways that must be considered for therapy to be effective.

Resistance is always present where there is oppression. When we pathologize or fail to recognize reactions to abuses of power as forms of resistance we miss oppor-tunities to build on existing efforts toward liberation. To offer a few examples, con-trolling one's sexual responses can be a form of resistance against being pressured into sex (invasion of personal space). I am thinking of couples with whom I have worked in which one is constantly pursuing and pressuring the other to have sex. The one being pursued avoids all contact for fear of being pressured. When an ad-vance occurs, the partner feeling pressured is often sexually shut down as a result of not feeling free to say no. I often tell couples that you should not say yes to sex until you are free to say no anytime for any reason. A child getting in the middle of an argument can be a form of resistance against oppression of a parent. For example, I recently supervised a case in which a 17-year-old daughter was acting out, frequent-ly yelling at and disobeying her father. The mother seemed unable or unwilling to contribute to setting limits, she herself feeling one down and overpowered by her husband. Many family therapists would point to the mother as the problem because she did not stand firm with her coparent. Another possibility emerged, however, as we considered the bond between the mother and daughter as a form of resistance to patriarchy. The daughter was in a safer position to speak out as a young woman nearing the point of leaving home. Other examples abound. Consider survivors of physical and sexual abuse who frequently report leaving their bodies as a way to escape while personal space is being violated. I often think of depression as a form of resistance against a partner's attempts to control.

Special Topic: Family Cartography

There are a number of tools for mapping relationships in family therapy includ-ing genograms, critical genograms, community genograms, structural family maps, maps of the problem's influence, maps of social capital, family drawings, life maps, and eco-maps. What I am proposing here is a way to capture family life within the spaces family members inhabit in order to better understand the relationship between power, privacy, personal space, social interactions, safety, and the problems presented in therapy.

I am suggesting the use of a topological map to portray themes that are relevant within meaningful space. Scale is not important and maps can be creatively and loosely drawn. The main point is to raise critical awareness by visually capturing how systems of power and privilege play out in relational and physical space. The following questions are examples of what therapists might ask during the process. They reflect attention to power, privacy, personal space, social interactions, safety, mobility, oppression, resistance, and resilience. The following questions (Fig. 6.1) and example (Fig. 6.2) map a family of origin, however questions can be easily altered to fit contemporary settings.

Case Example: My Family Map

What follows is a shortened example of my family of origin family cartography based on some of the questions listed above. I grew up in Flagstaff, Arizona, USA in the 1950s and 1960s. Flagstaff was a relatively small town at an elevation of 7000 ft. We moved to Flagstaff when my father secured financial backing to start a business (white privilege and male privilege) using his invention for turning Ponderosa Pine into pulp using mechanical rather than chemical processes. My father's invention was driven by Flagstaff's refusal to allow industries to use chemical pollutants (citizen-driven decision making). Local decisions like these maintained clean air and water for all citizens (democratic clean space). We lived in the woods North of the city, which left us isolated from daily social interaction with friends. My father's decision (male privilege, patriarchy) to move from Phoenix to Flagstaff also isolated my mother from the emotional support of my invalid grandmother who could not survive in high altitudes.

Flagstaff was more or less drawn into quarters with train tracks and Route 66 dividing north and south and a hill dividing east and west. North and Northwest Flagstaff was privileged space in which white, upper middle and middle class families occupied single-family dwellings with access to good schools, markets, and parks. The San Francisco Peaks were to the north along with the Museum of Northern Arizona. Our home was North of Flagstaff. Our 5 acres were surrounded by national Forest Service land, which provided seemingly endless acres of free public space for us as children to wander safely into our own imaginations. East Flag was a newer lower class development and home to many Mexican American and working-class white families. African Americans were segregated South of the train tracks. The Southeast Flag was home to the industrial area and my father's businesses. The impact of this industrial park was far from our home (spatial injustice). Most Navajos and Hopis whose ancestors once occupied all of this space—on whose land Flagstaff now sits—lived on reservations to the East (spatial and social injustice) and frequented Front Street on Route 66 for trade. There were also dorms

1. Describe the setting – physical environment, climate, town and neighborhood - in which you grew up. (Map the territory.)

2. What kinds of social interactions were available to you in this setting? Where were you and your family able to go and not go in this setting? How safe did you feel? What level of privacy and personal space did this setting provide?

3. Describe the power dynamics in this setting. Include race, class, gender, sexual orientation, abilities, nation of origin, language and any other signifiers that are relevant. (Add these to the map using symbols.)

4. How did these power dynamics affect you and your family? In what ways did you and/or your family members participate in the oppression or marginalization of others? How were you and your family oppressed or marginalized?

5. Describe the home in which you lived. (Add to map as an excerpt) What kinds of social interactions were available to you in and around your home? In what areas of the home did you spend the most time and why? Where were you able to go and not go in your home and why? How safe did you feel in various spaces in your home? What level of privacy and personal space did this setting provide?

6. Who was in your family? Who had the most power? How was the power enacted? (Draw a map excerpt to show family.) How do these power dynamics reflect the broader power dynamics in your community?

7. What spaces on your map reflect sites of oppression? Describe the relationships in these sites. (Add oppression symbols to the map.)

8. Where are sites of resistance? Describe the relationships in these sites. (Add resistance symbols to the map.) How did you and/or your family resist oppression? Where, what and how did you learn to resist oppression?

9. What types of resiliency did you develop as a result of this geography? (Add resilience symbols to the map.)

10. What else would you like to add to the map?

Fig. 6.1 Examples of questions for family cartography

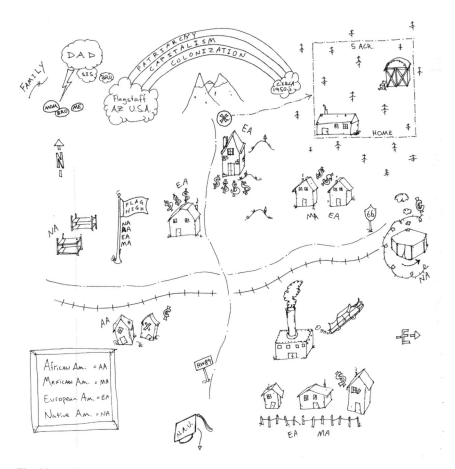

Fig. 6.2 My family map

for Navajo and Hopi kids near the West Flag high school (colonization). The West Flag high school was highly diverse relative to race, ethnicity, and social class. The racial discrimination of the broader society was reflected in the fact that white kids were dominant in nearly all aspects of student government even though we made up only 40 % of the student body. Patriarchs headed all the families I knew. Same sex parent and single female-headed families were all but invisible.

Northern Arizona University was on the far South border of Flagstaff. Having a University meant our small town offered plays, symphonies, and educational opportunities typically reserved for urban spaces. Because of my father's position in the community I was able to attend the university elementary and preschools (white privilege and class privilege). By the time I was 8 years old I was aware of my white, USA, middle-class class privilege. I was also becoming painfully aware of the pervasive presence of racism, sexism, and what I now understand as homophobia that saturated my daily life. I remember only one same sex family that was outed by rumors that swirled around their deeply marginalized children.

The interior space of our large home shifted across moments of significant oppression, resistance, privilege, and freedom. When my mother and brothers and I were home, the space was filled with creativity, humor, and fun (resistance and resilience). When my father was home, the space quickly shifted to dangerous territory that required us to be on alert to my father's surveillance and abusive control (patriarchy, male privilege, and sexism). My sister often served in a role of surveillance and control in my father's absence (patriarchy by proxy). There were spaces in the basement, formal living room, closets, and outside that provided cover. The barn was on the far side of our property and rarely visited by anyone but my brothers and myself, providing us a haven safe from family turmoil (spaces of resistance). The following map (Fig. 6.2) describes this narrative in visual form.

Implications for Practice

Family cartography can raise social awareness, encourage insight into relationship dynamics, and increase understanding of self and others. Methods of resistance can be identified and repertoires of resistance broadened. Resilience can be acknowledged and amplified. For example, my own map above sheds light on the multiplicity and complexity of privilege and oppression I experienced growing up. Discussions about this map might raise my awareness of my racism, internalized sexism, white privilege, homophobia, and classism. I would see the relationship between the privilege my family experienced and the oppression of others. I would hopefully realize the privilege of growing up with clean air and water, in safe places, with adequate indoor and outdoor space, and access to good education and other community resources. This would begin to balance a myopic view of the oppression I would likely recognize within my family if using only a genogram or structural map. The mapping exercise would help me connect the power dynamics within our home with the power dynamics in the broader society in a specific time and place. Looking at the forms of resistance that I commonly use when faced with attempts by others to overpower can be linked to what I learned about resistance early in my life. For example, I tended to accommodate or withdraw then and I tend to accommodate or withdraw now. Finally, the geography of my youth points to resilience I continue to access through solitude, play and humor when in safe spaces, determination, and flexibility.

Family cartography is only one way for family therapists to access the dimension of space to raise critical consciousness in support of social and relational equity. Therapists need to get into the habit of asking families about their homes, neighborhoods and communities. We need to know the geography and history of the cities in which we work and the related issues of spatial justice. When families tell stories, we can ask them to include the surroundings—what places were like. This deepens our understanding of context and family members' understanding of each other.

We need to explore the ways power dynamics in societies and communities are reflected in power dynamics in the family; how these contribute to the use of space, sense of safety in the home, freedom or lack of freedom in movement. In this chapter, I have only begun to explore the potential impact of placing space alongside time as a crucial element of the time–space interaction framework in the practice of family therapy. It is my hope that the dimension of space will open new doors for our collective work.

References

Almeida, R., Dolan-Del Vecchio, K., & Parker, L. (2007). *Transformative family therapy: Just families in a just society*. Boston: Allyn & Bacon.

Anzaldua, G. (2007). *Borderlands: La Frontera* (3rd ed.). San Fransisco: Aunt Lute Books.

Bourdieu, P. (1986). The forms of capital. In J. G. Richardson (Ed.), *Handbook of theory and research for the sociology of education* (pp. 241–258). New York: Greenwood Press.

Callis, A. (2014). Bi-sexual, pansexual, queer: Non-binary identities in the sexual borderlands. *Sexualities, 17*(1/2), 63–80. doi:10.1177/1363460713511094.

Einstein, Z. (1998). *Global obscenities: Patriarchy, capitalism, and the lure of cyberfantasy*. New York: New York University Press.

Fitzpatrick, K., & MaGlory, M. (2000). *Unhealthy places: The ecology of risk in the urban landscape*. New York: Routledge.

Gilliom, J. (2001). *Overseers of the poor: Surveillance, resistance, and the limits of privacy*. Chicago: University of Chicago Press.

Giroux, H. (2014). *Neolibralism's war on higher education*. Chicago: Haymarket Books.

Harding, S. (2008). *Sciences from below: Feminisms, postcolonialities, and modernities*. Durham: Duke University Press.

Harvey, D. (2001). *Spaces of capital: Towards a critical geography*. New York: Routledge.

Hertlein, K., & Ancheta, K. (2014). Advantages and disadvantages of technology in relaitonships: Findings from an open-ended survey. *The Qualitative Report, 19*(22), 1–11.

Hudson, C. (2012). Disparities in the geography of mental health: Implications for social work. *Social Work, 57*(2), 107–119. doi:10.1093/sw/sws001.

Jensen, A. (2011). Mobility, space and power: On the multiplicities of seeing mobility. *Mobilities, 6*(2), 255–271.

Soja, E. (2010). *Seeking spatial justice*. Minneapolis: University of Minnesota Press.

Tohe, L. (2007). Hweeldi Beehaniih: Remembering the long walk. *Wicazo Sa Review, 22*(1), 77.

Chapter 7
Practicing Critical Decolonizing Family Therapy

This chapter might be more aptly titled: "Critical and decolonizing theories are really interesting, I get it! But how do they actually apply to doing family therapy?" This is the question with which I am most often faced as a family therapy educator and supervisor. I typically answer that being able to understand multiple societal systems of power and oppression and how these influence our most intimate lives is not new to family therapy. That is what we do as systemic, contextual thinkers. It is necessary in order for us to be able to conceptualize problems and the impact of power dynamics within families and couples. That is what the previous chapters in this volume have been about.

I also point out that there are models of family therapy that already center analysis of power and goals of relational equity as central for individual and relational well-being. We need to learn from those already practicing this framework. The cultural context model (Almeida et al. 2007), just therapy (Waldegrave and Tamasese 1994), feminist family therapy (e.g., Prouty Lyness and Lyness 2007), and socioemotional relationship therapy (Knudson-Martin and Huenergardt 2010) are a few examples of highly developed models with techniques for using critical theory in practice.

In this chapter I invite family therapists to consider how we might further integrate critical decolonizing perspectives into our everyday work. I take the opportunity to expand on the question of how to apply critical decolonizing theory to family therapy by arguing that third-order, transformational change is a central, trans-theoretical goal in the practice of critically informed family therapy, and that transformational change can be integrated into practice across family therapy models. I suggest some guiding principles for critical decolonizing family therapy and apply these principles to a case example.

© American Family Therapy Academy 2015
T. McDowell, *Applying Critical Social Theories to Family Therapy Practice,*
AFTA SpringerBriefs in Family Therapy, DOI 10.1007/978-3-319-15633-0_7

Transformation

Family therapists talk a great deal about first- and second-order change. We are keen to create second-order change—change that makes a real and lasting difference. Change that occurs on different levels or stages has also been considered in critical theory and liberation-based work. In this section I make connections between Bateson's (1972) early systems thinking about levels of learning; commonly held ideas in family therapy about first-, second-, and third-order change; Soja's (2010) first, second, and third space; Freire's (1970) steps toward critical consciousness; and Laenui's (2006) phases of decolonization.

In *Steps to an Ecology of Mind* (1972), Bateson described levels of learning that serve as precursors to concepts of first-, second-, and third-order change:

> Learning I is change in specificity of response by correction of errors of choice within a set of alternatives. Learning II is change in the process of Learning I, e.g., a corrective change in the set of alternatives from which choice is made, or it is a change in how the sequence of experience is punctuated. Learning III is change in the process of Learning II, e.g., a corrective change in the system of sets of alternatives from which choice is made. (p. 298)

More simply put, level one or first-order change includes solutions to problems without changing the way problems are understood. These common sense solutions make no real difference to the organization of relationships. For example, a father may demand his son become like himself—in charge, successful, autonomous. First-order change includes the father trying a number of avenues to get through to his son including advising, encouraging, or demeaning him. The son may also try a number of responses such as working hard, becoming expert at something his father does not approve of, or simply giving up. First-order change can be useful in therapy when clients are in crisis or other situations that require a high degree of structure. The goal in these situations is to stabilize rather than necessarily promote lasting change. The schemas of the relationship dynamics stay intact (Bartunek and Moch 1987). Level 2 learning or second-order change requires looking at the pattern or process level of the relationship—reflecting and moving toward a different schema (Bartunek and Moch 1987). The double bind of the father telling the son to be like himself—that is someone who determines his own direction and tells others what to do—traps them in a logic error. Change at this level requires choosing from a different set of alternatives and/or punctuating the relationship differently. This might include interventions such as talking about intergenerational patterns and gender roles, reframing the father's demands as his way of nurturing, or looking for exceptions when the son is able to follow his own best judgment. Second-order change is what we typically aim for in therapy to help families make lasting significant change in the organization of their relationships.

Level 3 learning or third-order change requires a meta-perspective that considers the system of sets of alternatives—realizing and choosing between schemas (Bartunek and Moch 1987). This level of learning and change reveals meta-processes and meta-narratives. At this level the father and son connect their interaction to a much larger social pattern of patriarchy. Realizing the system of patriarchy and its influences requires viewing from outside or beyond, which in turn allows them to step out and not participate in patriarchy in the same way and/or to consider alternative systems of gender relations. Third-order change is associated with major shifts in the way clients see the world and their lives (Laurel and Hulley 1996).

Soja (2010) introduced the concept of first, second, and third space. First space is what structures and physical things there are in specific geographical locations. For example, as I write I am in my favorite chair, in my small home in a quiet neighborhood in a progressive city near where I work. Change in first space includes things like remodeling my kitchen. Second space builds on first space by describing my home beyond its structure and location; who lives there, where we eat and sleep, when the dog goes out, and what typically happens in this space. Home is free space for me as there are few interruptions or demands on my time. My home is filled with objects that elicit a lifetime of memories of places I have lived. Trees overshadow the yard, which allow me to feel insulated from others, privately tucked into my space.

Third space adds to understanding and possibilities at a more meta-level. There is a public park across the street and a public school a few houses away. My street is being overrun by businesses as they encroach into neighborhood space. My house is one of only a few left that are residential, situated in contested space representative of competition at a larger scale between public interest (parks and schools), for-profit endeavors (businesses), and private space (single dwelling homes). From a third space view, the safety and privacy of my home offer a protected area for imagining new ways of thinking and doing even within this context. For Soja, third space includes borderlands and places of resistance where more just relationships can be imagined and action toward social justice (social change) can be planned.

While Freire argued that there is no single process for conscientização, he observed several steps in critical consciousness (Afuape 2012). At first, people feel powerless to change their lives and try their best to conform to the way things are (i.e., first-order change). Antonio Gramsci used the term "common sense" to describe this type of thinking, which reflects not fully comprehending one's own oppression (Jones 2006). Next, people begin to see problems in their lives in terms of power relations, but on a local interpersonal level. There is greater understanding that specific people and relationships are unjust and a growing ability to change these relationships (i.e., second-order change). Finally, people recognize unjust relationships as embedded in systemic, institutionalized power structures (i.e., third-order change). Action to change unjust systems then becomes the focus.

Laenui (2006) outlined five interrelated, often overlapping, and co-occurring phases of decolonization. At first those who have been colonized are highly susceptible to viewing themselves as inferior to colonizers who have dominated in part through framing their culture as superior. Laenui did not include a type 1 change; however, this is easily implied as typically occurring through colonization. Change in this phase could be considered first order as it occurs within a colonizing framework. During phases of *rediscovery and recovery,* there is a growing awareness of the process of colonization and its damaging effects. Adopting aspects of traditional culture may be deeply reflected or somewhat superficial such as participating in

Table 7.1 Transformative change across theoretical frameworks

Theoretical framework	Type 1 change	Type 2 change	Type 3 change
Bateson's levels of learning	Change within existing schema	Change in schema	Change in meta-perspectives of schemas
First-, second-, third-order change	Common sense change within existing relational dynamics	Change that alters patterns of interaction, meaning	Transformative change in how we see and act in the world
Soja's first, second, third space	Change in physical space	Change in interactions, experience, meaning	Social change, imagining, resisting
Freire's steps in conscientização	Change that conforms to existing power structures	Change in power dynamics at relational level	Change in unjust societal systems
Laenui's processes of decolonization	Change within colonial framework	Change in meta view—rediscovery and recovery, mourning, and dreaming	Commitment and action; reclaiming indigenous worldview and practices; deliberate choice of hybrids in borderlands

traditions without changing one's worldview. Mourning is associated with discovering the damage colonization has caused. Laenui considers the phase of *dreaming* to be the most important for decolonization. Dreaming allows for possibilities, imagining a wide range of what can be. It provides opportunities for weighing ideas and voices. These changes in worldview and meaning-making could be considered second-order change. This process eventually leads individuals and communities to *commitment* toward carrying out shared dreams. Finally, this commitment leads to *action* toward decolonizing transformation, or what could be considered third-order change (Table 7.1).

While stage and phase theories have been heavily critiqued as oversimplifying processes that are neither linear nor categorically discrete, recognizing the correlation between levels of learning, orders of space and change, steps associated with conscientização and processes of decolonization can help align family therapy theory and models with liberation-based practices.

Toward Critical Decolonizing Family Therapy

Taking a critical decolonizing approach includes setting some common goals across family therapy models. Integrating critical decolonizing theories into existing family therapy models is beyond the scope of this volume. It is possible, however, to consider themes for practicing from critical decolonizing perspectives. First, those working from a critical decolonizing framework attempt to create third-order transformational change that addresses inequities seen as foundational to emotional and relational problems. Third-order change—as described above—involves change in meta-perspectives of schemas. This requires therapists and clients to be able to step back from their lives and see the ways we are all embedded in complex social systems. Once we see our worlds differently, more critically, we are able to take action that can solve presenting problems and increase equity in our relationships. Second, critical decolonizing therapy aims to create what Soja (2010) described as third space for change where we can imagine new ways of being and engaging in our worlds. Care is taken not to recreate unjust social arrangements in therapy, for therapy to disrupt rather than support cultural hegemony (see McDowell, Chap. 1, this volume). Third, therapists add the dimension of space to time as a means of supporting spatial justice alongside time-dependent patterns and stories. Fourth, critical decolonizing efforts challenge dominant discourses and/or rhetoric that attribute social inequities to a natural order that favors those in power, instead validating lived experience and supporting authentic equitable relationships.

Case Example

Juan and David entered therapy after one of their many arguments resulted in David leaving for several days. David came from an upper class, white family and was employed as a school administrator. Juan was a first generation Mexican immigrant who came to the USA to work as a laborer out of economic need. While the couple received expensive gifts from David's family, Juan regularly sent money home. Juan came across as traditionally masculine and chose to identify as heterosexual, gay, or bi-sexual in various contexts of his life. David identified as gay and gender variant. The common conflation of gender expression and sexual orientation led most people to assume he was gay. Juan was younger and more attractive than David. In the course of therapy it became clear that while the relationship was important to both, David was highly invested in making it work and sensitive to Juan's opinion. David felt more satisfied and reported being happier together than did Juan. Juan was slow to offer David his approval and affection. David would often set the agenda and make major decisions that affected them both. When these decisions resulted in arguments, Juan repeated his points and escalated before turning away from David, perceiving David as not hearing him. In turn, David would feel disrespected and dismissed before threatening to leave the relationship. The couple would fight until they eventually dropped the topic or compromised.

David and Juan's relationship reflected the nuances of power found in most couples. David's social position as a white, male professional from an upper class US family afforded him greater privilege and power in the relationship. While he deeply cared about Juan, he was less attuned to Juan's needs, often assuming he knew what would be best for them both. He wanted to please Juan, but on his own terms. David was relatively unaware of his privileged position and was surprised to discover that Juan routinely accommodated his wishes. Juan escalated and repeated his arguments in an attempt to elicit empathy and understanding from David. David interpreted this as nagging, paying less and less attention to bids for understanding as anger escalated.

Encouraging Third-Order Transformation

As with any situation, Juan and David's relationship can be viewed from a variety of perspectives. Therapists using various family therapy models would punctuate their problems and solutions differently. Hopefully, the various avenues for helping the couple move forward would all lead to positive outcomes. Would these outcomes support first-, second-, or third-order change? Would Juan and David be offered the opportunity to transform their relationship? Using a critical decolonizing lens would provide the therapist and the couple with a framework to reconsider the relational dynamics not only from a meta-perspective, but from a perspective that allows the couple the opportunity to decide between schemas. They could choose a more just structure that relies on power sharing. Juan and David would gain a better understanding of how social schemas of patriarchy, colonization, and capitalism produce homophobia, sexism, racism, and Nationism, which in turn influence their family of origin and shared couple schemas. They would understand each other's emotions not only at a personal level, but through a lens that provides social relational context (Knudson-Martin and Huenergardt 2010) to their experience and the feelings they express to each other.

Creating a Third Space for Change

Third space is made in therapy by inviting reflection, imagining just relationships, and developing strategies for change. A critical decolonizing lens requires that we find ways to address power when we work with families. Critical conversations in family therapy (Korin 1994) are based on the work of emancipatory educator Paulo Freire (1970). According to Freire, dialogue and reflection that lead to informed action is central to raising critical consciousness, or conscientização. Building on this tradition, Martin-Baro (1994, p. 40) argued that "...people must take hold of their fate, take the reins of the lives, a move that demands overcoming false consciousness and achieving a critical understanding of themselves as well as of their world and where they stand in it." He echoed Freire's claims that through dialogue we are able to change our reality; through decoding our worlds we are able to understand the mechanisms of oppression and possibilities for action. These new understandings transform our social identities, increasing our agency to transform our lives. Raising social awareness requires us to reconnect with our legacies of privilege and oppression, our collective histories (Martin-Baro 1994).

Problem-posing questions often start with noticing something about our lives that reflects social inequity. According to Bartunek and Moch (1987), these questions often start with "how." For example, the therapist might ask Juan and David "How did you learn to be males in your family and culture?" "How was manhood associated with being attracted to women?" "How are families in Mexico and the United States affected by the border between the two countries?" Reflection questions often start with "why." For example, the therapist might ask David and Juan, "Why do you think being seen as masculine is important in your family? Community? Society?" "Why is it associated with being heterosexual?" "Why is race and nation of origin so influential in the U.S.?" Dialogue that continues to weave between problem posing and reflection leads to social and relational awareness, which in turn is necessary to successfully navigate change and action toward greater equity.

Adding the Dimension of Space to Time

The dimension of time is highly prioritized in family therapy. Therapists encourage clients to tell their stories, to look at the past and plan for the future. Rarely is attention paid to the dimension of space (see McDowell, Chap. 6, this volume). The dimension of space is influential in the power dynamic between Juan and David. It is not possible to understand their relationship without positioning this couple in a particular space. Juan likely experiences racism and Nationism as a Mexican immigrant. His family remains in Mexico and relies on his financial support he is able to provide by working in a more wealthy and powerful country. The history between the USA and Mexico includes ongoing spatial tension based on power and access to resources. Raising critical consciousness of spatial justice would help David and Juan team together in their care for Juan's family and efforts to create a more equal culturally situated relationship. The therapist might ask Juan and David about what differences they have noticed between the physical spaces in which they each grew up—in which each of their families live. The couple would be invited to explore how it is that there is such discrepancy in resources across countries; how national borders affect the status each holds in the US society. Juan and David would gain awareness of the influence of space on their relationship and the view others may have of their relationship.

Decolonizing Relational Dynamics

Critical decolonizing therapy challenges colonial agendas that center cultural, social, and symbolic capital of the most dominating groups in society (see McDowell, Chaps. 2 and 4, this volume). Privilege based on skin tone, language/accent, and social habits are just a few examples of how colonial processes might affect the power dynamics between David and Juan. Juan has several important resources that influenced his emotional well-being and power in the relationship, e.g., being more attractive which offered Juan more options outside the relationship and being able to withhold the approval David sought. Juan was lower status, however, based on the social hierarchy established by European dominance and colonization. David's class privilege both reflected and maintained his colonial privilege. David feels underappreciated for what he brings to the relationship, but Juan feels undervalued. Being emotionally vulnerable and attuned would become less difficult as David and Juan were able to examine the connection between larger social forces of colonization and their intimate power dynamics.

Conclusion: Next Steps

This volume would not be complete without at least a nod to the future of critical decolonizing theories in the practice of family therapy. As I see it we have several tasks ahead. First, we need to continue to search beyond our walls for meaningful, interdisciplinary knowledge that supports equity and family well-being. Failure to do so aggravates our risk of maintaining the status quo through our field's common knowledge and practices. Second, we should emphasize social awareness and the value of supporting equitable relationships in family therapy initial and continuing education. We need to teach equity-based family therapy models in training programs and integrate practical, hands-on methods of supporting social and relational equity into everyday supervision practices. Third, we need to continue to develop family therapy models that center on social and relational equity. Far from being neutral, failing to challenge current social arrangements promotes emotional and relational problems. Most importantly, we need to systematically infuse existing family therapy models with critical decolonizing approaches to change. This is a task in which my colleagues and I are currently engaged.

Overall, my goal for this volume is to promote the equity and well-being of individuals, couples, and families. My intention is to make critical decolonizing work more accessible in daily practice. My hope is that this body of work will inspire others, including new generations of family therapists to use their imaginations, their hearts, and their talents to build a more just society.

References

Afuape, T. (2012). *Power, resistance and liberation in therapy with survivors of trauma: To have our hearts broken*. New York: Routledge.

Almeida, R., Dolan-Del Vecchio, K., & Parker, L. (2007). *Transformative family therapy: Just families in a just society*. Boston: Allyn & Bacon.

Bartunek, J., & Moch, M. (1987). First-order, second-order, and third order change and organizational development interventions: A cognitive approach. *The Journal of Applied Behavioral Science, 23*(4), 483–500.

Bateson, G. (1972). *Steps to an ecology of mind: Collected essays in anthropology, psychiatry, evolution, and epistemology*. London: Jason Aronson Inc.

Freire, P. (1970). *Pedagogy of the oppressed*. New York: Continuum.

Jones, S. (2006). *Antonio Gramsci* (Routledge Critical Thinkers). New York: Routledge.

Knudson-Martin C., & Huenergardt, D. (2010). A socio-emotional approach to couple therapy: Linking social context and couple interaction. *Family Process, 49*(3), 369–384. doi:10.1111/j.1545-5300.2010.01328.x.

Korin, E. C. (1994). Social inequalities and therapeutic relationships: Applying Freire's ideas to clinical practice. *Journal of Feminist Family Therapy, 5*(3/4), 75–98.

Laenui, P. (2006). Processes of decolonization. http://www.sjsu.edu/people/marcos.pizarro/maestros/Laenui.pdf. Accessed 30 Nov 2014.

Laurel, B., & Hulley, E. (1996). *Depth oriented brief therapy*. San Francisco: Jossey Bass.

Martin-Baro, I. (1994). *Writings for a liberation psychology*. Cambridge: Harvard University Press.

Prouty Lyness, A., & Lyness, K. (2007). Feminist issues in couple therapy. *Journal of Couple & Relationship Therapy, 6*(1/2), 181–195.

Soja, E. (2010). *Seeking spatial justice*. Minneapolis: University of Minnesota press.

Waldegrave, C., & Tamasese, K. (1994). Some central ideas in the "Just Therapy" approach. *Family Journal, 2*(2), 94–103.

Made in the USA
Columbia, SC
20 August 2021